I Have Been a Fighter My Whole Life

Marie Scofield

Disclaimer

This story is based on the true events and unforgettable episodes in my life. Certain long-standing institutions, agencies, and public offices are mentioned as is, but for the sake of privacy, certain names of people in my life have been altered, and other identifying details have been omitted or exaggerated.

The opinions expressed here are my own, based on how I saw and experienced certain events. Please note that there is no desire to view or show anyone in a negative light. Any slight—perceived or imagined—is not intentional on my part.

Note from the Author

"Sometimes, even to live is an act of courage."

—Lucius Annaeus Seneca

Suicide not only affects you but also your dear loved ones, including friends and family. Once you hurt yourself, you will leave a scar on your body and soul and regret your decision to do it.

When you're in a dark place, never believe that you're alone. Please see and tell someone how you feel; do not hide your problems and burdens from your loved ones. Talk to them, even if you're only talking to your friends or family.

Suicide can seem like a black cloud with no sun coming through, but I promise you that every cloud has a silver lining. You just have to be able to see it shining through.

Love,

Marie Scofield

Suicide Helplines

If you or your loved ones are struggling with suicidal ideation, depression, or have thoughts about self-harm, please reach out to the support system and initiatives like Lifeline.

The Lifeline network provides free, confidential support focusing on prevention along with crisis resources for you or your loved ones.

If you're worried about a loved one or a friend or need some emotional support, you can call on the Lifeline network, which is available on a 24/7 basis.

The National Suicide Prevention Lifeline's number is 988, OR call on 1-800-273-8255.

The Crisis Text Line can be reached by texting HOME to 741741 (US), 686868 (Canada), or 85258 (UK).

Dedication

To my mother, who has always been there for me since day one. And my Muri family, who love me unconditionally and also believe that I will be successful. Lastly, to my best friends who supported me in becoming the author of this book.

Acknowledgments

I want to thank the people in my life right now who have supported me in my journey of writing this book and making my dream of becoming an author come true. If I had succeeded in ending my life, I would not have had the chance to write and share my story with others.

In 2020, I was struggling – going on and off about writing down the rough manuscript. I was almost going to give up on my book, but I realized that I should share my world as a deaf person with others. I wanted them to see the world through my eyes.

My final failed suicide attempt opened my eyes. I think my story will impact everyone going through a rough time, and I understand that if I can make it through, they can, too.

I am so excited to start the journey for this book for the first time.

Hello, publishing company. Thank you for taking the time to edit my book. Being an author is challenging in the first place, but with your help, I made it!

About the Author

After her final failed suicide attempt, Marie Scofield embraced her life, which inspired her to write this book and tell everyone how she is a fighter and finally accepted change. Sharing her life's story is a beautiful experience as she is also able to raise awareness on how people who are deaf or hard of hearing can change the world and the future.

Her inspiration to become an author was sparked in 2015 when she was in high school as a senior, and she watched a speech-deaf author publish her book. She was motivated to become an author one day, and her dream came true with her very first book.

Despite her attempts, Marie understands the plight of people driven to suicide and knows firsthand how harmful it can be for survivors, too. Marie's story will resonate with others having tough times in their lives.

Preface

I am Marie Scofield. I was born in Florida, in the city of Fort Myers. My parents are deaf, and I have one younger hearing sister. One rule I have always upheld in my life is, *"Trust your intuition always when you think it's wrong or when you know you have received the right answer."*

Being deaf doesn't stop me from doing anything and becoming successful. Being deaf is a challenging yet beautiful experience in the world; it can be a relief when you can't hear sounds.

I communicate by using sign language instead of speaking by lips. Sign language is my first language to share with family and other people. Don't assume that deaf people can't do anything because they can't hear any sound. That is not true, as I have done everything just like hearing people. I attended college, had a job, and more.

I am so proud to be part of the deaf community. I think that we should not let PTSD (Post Traumatic Stress Disorder) take over our lives. I'm saying this from experience. At my lowest points, I attempted suicide multiple times because I saw no other way out of the darkness that surrounded me. Thankfully, I failed each time!

Now that I have come out of that part of my life, I can assure you that just like everything, the darkness will pass as well. Still here, on this Earth, I can see that God has given me a chance to understand my life's purpose and how it will improve.

You see, I had a gift ever since I was born. I have been blessed with clairvoyance because I can always sense when something is about to happen. My prophecies started in high school and have become stronger with the passage of time.

This is why I always say, "Trust your intuition."

Your inner world inside you is very real and powerful. It compels you to see what is happening around the world with a clarity that can be terrifying.

How can you change in the future with everything when technology becomes more advanced and ruins the Earth?

It is already predicted that the way we are advancing will affect the economy badly in the future and destroy the homes of animals. The question then becomes as to how we can survive in this bad economy.

It is apparent that we need to learn survival skills like growing our own produce such as fruits and vegetables. We can also see how our bodies become healthier when we switch to a plant-based diet and become aware of the way the world is changing!

Contents

Chapter 1: My Birth Story

I was born on January 27, 1996, in Fort Myers Health Park Hospital, around 6:14 a.m. I was just two pounds and eight ounces, and my birth was sudden and untimely. I came into this world without fully maturing in my mother's womb.

Since birth, I have been a fighter because I was premature. Initially, I struggled to breathe and was hooked up to a machine that helped me stay alive. I had to stay at the hospital for two months so I could fully develop because of my early arrival into this world.

When I was inside my mother's belly, the doctor said I had been infected as my mother had a teeth condition, periodontitis. When my mother went to the hospital for her check-up, the doctor decided to check up on any other infections, but my mother's water actually broke during the examination, and I came out like a basketball.

To ensure that I survived, I was kept in the hospital until I got a little healthy.

My mother visited me daily and watched me grow and improve. When she had to feed me for the first time, she had to use syringes, and she was very nervous. At that time, a nurse helped my mother take care of me as well.

The nurse also told my mother I could be deaf because I didn't cry as much as a healthy baby did. One year later, my mother brought me to an audiologist to get an audiogram so they could check whether I was deaf or able to hear. An audiogram is a graph test that charts a person's hearing abilities based on the softest sounds one can hear. These sounds are played at different frequencies and pitches. All of this is done to test whether someone can hear or not.

The audiologist sedated me with a syrup medicine to help me sleep through the test because that would make it easier to identify my hearing range for them. However, the dosage they gave me was probably too strong because it made me stop breathing for some reason.

The nurse prayed for me with my mother, but luckily, my breathing returned to normal. Then, the audiologist administered the test, and the results were not good. He told my mother I was profoundly deaf.

People who are classified as profoundly deaf cannot hear anything at all. They're totally reliant on lip-reading or sign language to communicate. I grew up with sign language as my first language.

One day, my mother brought me to the doctor for an examination. The doctor said I had hemiplegia on my left side. Later, I discovered that the left side was just weaker because of one-sided muscle weakness, not paralysis.

The doctor asked my mother if I ate very well.

She answered, "Yes. Why?"

The doctor showed her how my health was being impacted. I was getting virtually no exercise. The doctor found out that my tummy had no muscles, and I needed to exercise daily to become stronger. If things did not improve, it was likely that my body would atrophy to the point where I would have to be fed from a tube and be in a wheelchair.

My mother agreed. She did not want to see me in a wheelchair. So, she worked hard on me so much that during the next follow-up appointment, the doctor observed my improvement, and he said, "You've done a good job, and you've successfully improved your daughter's health!"

I was told that I had to wear a brace on my left leg because my muscles were too weak. However, I did not wear this often because of my stubbornness. I also did not like the brace. I refused to listen, even when my mother tried to explain that it was for my own good.

My stubbornness came from the fact that in school, one of my classmates had cerebral palsy, and he had to wear a brace and push the mobility aid walker to get around. I did not feel like I had cerebral palsy. I was average and did not want to be like him.

I also underwent multiple surgeries, once at the age of three and again at seven years old, on my left ankle because of tendonitis. The muscle there was tight and reduced my mobility a lot, making it difficult for me to walk long distances.

Till the age of five, I saw a lot of domestic violence in my house. My father was extremely abusive toward my mother. He engaged in substance abuse, either drinking excessively or taking drugs to get high. He kept beating my mother for no reason when he was high or drunk.

My mother suffered for a long time until my father left our lives. I will never forget that my mother had almost died before my eyes when I was just five years old and my little sister was four. Back then, we moved from Fort Myers, Florida, to a new apartment in Cape Coral, Florida.

One evening, I didn't understand what was going on between my parents. They kept arguing, and the situation escalated until my father became insane and then decided to choke my mother. He wrapped his hands around her neck and kept squeezing until she passed out and slumped to the floor as she stopped breathing.

My little sister and I witnessed the whole scene unfold right in front of us. We were so afraid that we ran, hid inside the closet, and cried hard. Fortunately, someone had heard the commotion and called 911 because they thought my mother was in trouble.

Luckily, my mother regained consciousness and woke up in terror. She found me and my sister and hugged us. She stayed with us until the Police arrived and arrested my father.

I saw my dad as he was cuffed and escorted to the police car. He showed no remorse and did not care what he had done to my mother. I think all of this was because he had anger issues and would get angry over the smallest things. He also always wanted to be around drug addicts or crackheads.

He couldn't break his addiction, which warped his mindset. He never believed that family should come first or that he should be a good role model or dad to my sister and me. After he was jailed, my mother got a restraining order against him.

He couldn't be near us when he got out of jail and didn't return to us because of our mother's restraining order. I didn't see him again until the age of fifteen when he returned.

Chapter 2: Near Drowning

When I was around five years old, I was afraid of swimming by myself because I was scared of the water and still had PTSD from one particular incident.

One hot afternoon, I went to my mother's friend's house for a swim because they had a kiddie pool. I decided to join their older boys there. My mother's friend's son was playing rough with me. He had some other ideas in mind about what consisted of fun things to do in the water – he kept dunking me and putting my head down in the water. I struggled to get out and breathe, and he'd grab me and do it again when I'd get away from him.

Luckily, my mother and her friend were nearby and spotted him doing that. They dashed over to stop him. I cried hard and said I wouldn't play with him again because I felt he was mean to me, even though he insisted that he was playing with me. I did not think he was!

After the incident, when I revisited them, he apologized for what he had done to me and tried to cheerfully invite me to play with him in the kiddie pool again.

I kept saying no, and after that incident, I became rather fearful of swimming in public pools. I always preferred to be in pretty low water and where my feet could touch the ground, and I refused to go further. Anytime I stepped into deeper water, I would have severe flashbacks about what occurred to me and what the person had done.

Another time, I was at a hotel with my mother for her class reunion event. Curious, I made my way to the hotel pool and walked down the three steps. I held on to the metal railing, trying to feel the water temperature, but I slipped and accidentally fell in, and I could not swim out.

I struggled to swim, but I couldn't breathe, and I started to panic even more. I wanted to scream, and I started pulling my hair as I became disoriented because everything was so dark. I could see nothing underwater.

However, it was good that someone noticed I was in the water for longer than expected. Thankfully, they pulled me out. I came up gasping for air and spitting out the water that I had swallowed. After that, I was terrified to swim alone without assistance because the PTSD of the incident would hit me big time.

I was ten years old when I finally overcame my fear of swimming in deep water, and that happened while I was in a boarding school for the deaf. My Physical Education (PE) teacher threw me into the pool when I did not want to swim because I thought it would be deep, but I was wrong.

I still remember how I sat at the pool bench and watched other kids play and swim.

The teacher said, "Please go in the water and get some exercise."

I ignored their instruction, not because I wanted to but because I was scared. I couldn't stop trembling, and my body shook like a leaf. The teacher decided to grab me and throw me in the pool. I came up, spluttering and gasping, and as my feet touched the ground and I stood up, I realized the water was not as deep as I had thought.

Slowly, the teacher taught me how to swim correctly, and I overcame my fears. Today, I can swim anywhere without fear of the darkness.

Chapter 3: Doves

In March 2004, my maternal grandfather passed away. I didn't understand how it all happened so suddenly; he had a heart attack followed by a stroke. During his last few weeks, people had known that his time was coming. He couldn't remember who the family members were.

When he died, Mother and I saw so many white doves in front of our eyes that we couldn't even count them. I felt elated at the sight. When Mother and I rushed to leave the house and out the front door, we noticed the *doves* fly away.

It was stunning, and I cannot describe how I felt in one word.

I looked at my mother and said, "I know it is my grandpa's message telling us that he is at peace in heaven."

It was truly God's gift for me and my mother to see and share with our whole family. I will never forget that moment. I cherish it in my memories because it showed me that heaven is real.

One month later, our family went to Pennsylvania in late April for another funeral. I did not watch other family members give a speech in the church because I did not understand what was being said. There was no interpreter present, and I also have attention deficit hyperactivity disorder (ADHD), which made it difficult for me not to sit and stay still for hours on end.

Additionally, I had not taken my medicines in the morning because I could only eat them after breakfast. Foolishly, I thought I'd be fine without them until I got myself breakfast. Normally, if I did take meds without breakfast, the drugs would make my stomach hurt and make me feel nauseous.

After the funeral, we gathered to go see Grandpa's grave, pay our respects to him, and visit the graves of other dead family members of the past. When the funeral was over, we stayed in Pennsylvania for a few days before heading to Florida.

The weather was cold, and we stayed indoors most of the time because of the rain. It was boring; all I could do was watch TV and play with the toy I got for Easter. Later on, I got to go to the railroad museum tour, take a train, and get some beef jerky and pretzel that was famous in the state.

"I can smell Grandpa's cologne around you," my Aunt Belle told me.

I knew he was protecting me with his spirit at the time and later on, anywhere I went, even when I returned to Florida and went back to school. About a few months later, I visited my aunt's house to give her some paperwork to complete.

I always felt excited to see Grandpa and say "I love you" to him in sign language and sometimes hop on his lap for a cuddle. He did not know all sign language and only knew how to say "LOVE" in sign language.

When I entered the house, I saw the chair where Grandpa preferred to sit and watch the television. The empty chair made me miss him, his scent, and his cooking when he made delicious meals for the family.

I knew he was at peace in heaven with his loved ones, friends, and family. Once I saw a dove, I knew he was at peace at the time. I will never forget how great he was. He raised his twelve children and loved and supported them unconditionally.

Before Grandpa went to heaven, my favorite memory was that he had his fruit supply trees, such as mangoes, oranges, bananas, and lemons. I would always go to the orange tree and eat my fill, consuming an unlimited amount until I felt too full to eat. Grandpa loved to feed the bird with seed and the squirrel with nuts. When Mother and I saw a dove, it represented his love for birds. I believe that heaven sent those doves to wait outside to make me and Mother see it.

We only saw it once in our lives and never again in the future.

Chapter 4: Sexual Abuse Victim

When I was around ten years old, my mother's boyfriend sexually abused me. The man did horrible things to me and then scared me so that I would not tell anyone about this incident or where and when it occurred.

As I silenced myself, it felt like I was suffocating. All the hurt, anguish, and pain burrowed inside me, deepening the wounds he had created ,which eventually led me to commit suicide. But now, I don't need to be silent anymore.

I can share the incident here.

The first time I tried to commit suicide was in 2006, two years before my grandfather passed away. I was going through a lot of emotional turmoil and was also not performing well in school. I didn't know how to deal with everything. Feeling overwhelmed, I thought this was my only way out.

Someone called the hotline about my situation and explained how I'd been molested repeatedly by a man. I think I also told the counselor about the situation with my mother's boyfriend after my suicide attempt on the playground.

I'd decided to take all my shoe's lace and tie it to a pole from which I would hang myself. The staff rushed to me, removed the shoelaces, and brought me to the counselor's office to figure out what could have caused me to act this way. It took a long time, but I finally opened up and told them everything.

I thought nothing would come off it, and as I was trying to pick up the pieces and move on, one Friday, my mother came. I saw her standing there as I rode the bus to Fort Myers after school. My mother was standing outside with a woman who, I later found out, was from child protective services.

I was so happy to see her. I got off the bus and rushed to her, thinking she'd come to take me home.

"You have to go with this woman," Mother told me.

"Why?" I asked her.

"It's hard to explain," she said. "You don't need to know the details."

It turns out that the child protective services were investigating the charges, and until then, she was not allowed to be near me. I stayed temporarily at someone's house for one night, and the following day, the worker took me to Mia's house—my mother's friend; she is deaf, too.

Despite that, I didn't feel comfortable because I was staying there for a few weeks indefinitely. I wanted to go home to my mom, and I didn't know when I would get to do that.

During my stay with Mia, I realized that a few things there were not like usual because she decided to contact my father on the computer.

Additionally, I was tired of staying at her place. I missed attending school but couldn't attend classes because I was so sick at Mia's house; I kept throwing up and didn't know why. I guess I just felt sick because of the stress I was under and due to the homesickness. I feel like I had food poisoning because I could smell and taste a rotten egg. I was also throwing up, mostly after I ate lunch.

Up till this point, no one really knew what was happening. My mother had told no one else in the family. However, later, my mother went to court to drop off critical paperwork pertaining to my case. She didn't realize that my cousin, Kara, also worked there and left the forms with her without saying a word and walked out.

So, it was no surprise that after work, cousin Kara immediately told Aunt Belle about what was going on. A few days later, I felt a lot better, and my bout of food poisoning was almost over. Mia's son, Jace, who is deaf too, took me back to the Florida School for the Deaf and the Blind. I only stayed there three days a week, which was so short for me.

With so much change happening around me, I was severely emotional, depressed, and upset because I didn't understand what was happening and why I couldn't see Mom. However, my dorm staff, Joa, tried to comfort me.

"Everything will be okay," she told me.

I saw the counselor often, usually off-campus. Her name was Chole. She was a sweet lady with blonde hair who gave me a photo of her and her dog together.

Going to the counselor during this time was extremely helpful because, finally, I could talk. I could let out all the unspoken words that had been festering inside me, eating me up alive.

I vented a lot to her about what happened between my mother's boyfriend and I. Chole understood how I felt, not just relating to the sexual abuse but the turmoil it caused in my life. Another thing I liked about Chloe was that sometimes, she and I would just play different board games together.

While things were going well in school, they remained the same, more or less at home. I started hating Friday rides on the bus back home because I did not want to see Mia. I was not doing well under her care.

Then, Mom told me something that made me so happy.

"You are going to stay at Aunt Belle's house," she told me.

I was so relieved. What delighted me even more was that Mom asked if she could come over and wait until I went to bed, and the worker approved it. I was going to stay at my aunt's house for one month.

During this time, my mom kept fighting CPS to get me back. She attended every court hearing and met all their requirements, and then one day, the judge told her that she could have her daughter back and I would be returned home.

She cried tears of joy and was happy that it was all resolved so quickly and that she did not have to go through more cases and court hearings.

Chapter 5: Bully

One evening, at around 8:30 p.m., I decided to escape from my dorm. I don't know why I picked that evening because there was a pretty bad storm happening with a lot of heavy rain and lightning. It felt like the right time because I assumed the storm would mask any sounds I made and keep everyone distracted.

After making sure that the coast was clear, I zoomed out the door, but I was caught. Joa, one of the staff members, saw me and started to chase after me. She feared the worst because I'd confided to her how I'd start to get fed up with my life.

I also experienced depression, and my self-esteem was low. This was due to the fact that another student was insulting me about a wart that had appeared on both of my hands. They liked to make fun of it, but more than that, they liked to see me get mad and get punished when I retailed.

Then, they'd pretend that they were perfectly innocent. I was the one who was displaying wrong or aggressive behavior. That evening, when I decided to make a run for it, I'd reach my limit. I could no longer take their cruel words anymore.

I ran outside in my pajamas and without any shoes. It was raining so much that I was instantly soaked.

Barefoot, I ran to another building that was right across the dorm. It was for elementary students.

I stood by the door because I was out of breath from running in the run. This allowed Joa to finally catch up to me. Quickly, she picked me up with one hand while I tried to break free from her grasp. She brought me back with my feet kicking.

When we returned to the dorm, she made me change my clothes and go to sleep. As punishment, I was grounded and stayed in the room for the rest of the night without going to watch the television with the rest of the girls.

The next morning, I woke up, and as I ate breakfast, the other students mocked me about last night's incident.

"I thought you would die after getting hit by lightning, but you're fine!" one girl said.

I didn't say anything. Instead, I finished up my meal and walked to the classroom. As I sat down at my desk, I felt a huge sinking feeling. I didn't want to do the assignment, but I still made myself do it.

*****

Another day, I had enough and escaped from the classroom to go outside. What happened was that my teacher pulled me out of the classroom and made me stand in the hallway. They planned to talk with me about my behavior and how what I was doing wasn't acceptable.

Standing out in the hallway by myself, I realized that I didn't want to stay. I looked at the stairs and seeing no one there, I decided to run to the hallway and go outside. With that in mind, I raced down the stairs as fast as possible.

My teacher saw me and chased after me. Seeing that I would get in further trouble, I decided to stop and let them escort me back to the building. I still earned a visit to the principal's office for trying to run away.

Reluctantly, I went to see the principal.

"Your actions have big consequences," she told me. "You must stay back from lunch and stay in detention all day."

During this time, I had to finish all the assignments the teacher gave me that I was slacking. It took me four hours to finish it, and I also made up for it during the lunch break.

"You must also stay home for a week."

That meant I got to miss the event, a Valentine's Day party arranged at school.

When I was at home with my mom, I cried hard because I wanted to leave the boarding school for good. I really hated going there. Since I had no friends, I was always being bullied and picked on, and the other kids also called me different names and hurt my feelings.

I always told my mother everything, so I even informed her about the incident in the school and what caused this to happen.

"Be strong and ignore what others say," she said. "You are smart, and that is important. Focus on the assignment and get good grades."

Her words inspired me because I know she told me the truth, and what she said was for my own good.

Chapter 6: Middle School

I clearly remember the first day of my sixth grade at the Fort Myers Middle Academy. I had to wear a uniform following their dress code policy. I was nervous because it was my first year in a hearing school. I did meet all my teachers during the open house.

However, I was confident because I was selected to take classes with mainstream students. But I didn't have any classes with deaf students due to their intelligence level.

On the first day of school, my teacher, who taught deaf students, tagged everyone to introduce themselves.

There was another young girl there who the teacher said was named Marilee. I tried to find her in the room and said, "Who?"

Marilee waved to me, and I replied, "Oh, you are Marilee?"

We chatted and got along so well despite the fact that I was nervous because we'd just met for the first time.

Soon, the bell rang for math class. I watched all the other students leave, and for some reason, I decided I wouldn't leave the room.

However, my teacher said, "You have to go."

I still refused. I did engage in rebellious behavior and could be pretty stubborn when I wanted to. The teacher became frustrated with me and said, "You need to leave the room. Now."

I complied, but I thought it was unfair. When school was finished for the day, I got home and told my mother and godmother about it because I wanted to stay with the deaf student because I got used to having other classmates like me in a deaf school.

I missed my fifth-grade classes and experiences, which is why I was not aware of the sixth-grade levels yet.

Marilee and I had similar classes together. We became best friends quickly and always talked too much in class. The teacher always got annoyed about it. She would say, "Do you and Marilee want to get a separate table and seat?"

We'd answer no and start to get serious about our lesson.

Out of all my funny and favorite memories together, the one I recall the most is when we got in trouble and had to go to the detention room. I got in trouble due to giving attitude to a teacher. This was because we hadn't done assignments or schoolwork. Instead, we would sit next to each other and talk too much to the point where others would tell us to stop and focus on the schoolwork.

Marilee and I became very close friends. We talked about anything and everything together. After school, we would also hang out at her house or mine for the weekend and do a lot of fun things together.

In September 2009, when I was thirteen years old, I was arrested for the first time and registered as a juvenile on the domestic violence list. When I was on the bus, that's when I liked to do all my homework before getting home. I tended to do that instead of doing it at home because, at that time, I'd just want to relax or eat dinner and chat with my godmother on a video phone call to talk about how my day was going.

However, my mother assumed that because I wasn't doing any work at home, I wasn't doing anything at all. She wouldn't let me talk with my godmother on video chat. Instead, she said, "Please do your homework."

I told her honestly, "I swear everything is completed. I did it on the bus when I was on it for at least one hour."

However, when she refused to believe me or listen to me, I got very frustrated. Things escalated to the point where my mother and I got into a bad fight because I got angry, and even though I did not mean to, I pulled my mother's hair. We were making so much noise that our neighbors decided to call the Police on us.

When I found out that the Police were arriving, I felt guilty and decided to go inside and lock the door because I could tell I would get arrested. So, I tried to tell the Police that I felt calmer now and wanted to resolve the issue with my mother. I don't know how the Police opened the door, but my sister acted as my interpreter.

She told me to remain calm and let the Police cuff me and then to go in the car. I was too upset and cried in the car because I thought my life would be over. I had just started sixth grade, and I was in middle school and trying to adjust to living with my family rather than staying at the deaf boarding school.

In the police car, I felt too anxious. When they took me to the police station, I saw many different adults and juveniles with various skin colors.

"Stand on the wall to get your picture taken," the officer told me.

It was all done very quickly. The Police do not have time to get a perfect picture like schools do on picture day or some other event. The Police led me outside to a cell and kept me there until my next processing step.

I was still in my school uniform, and my hair was too messy. I sat in the cell and had a lot of thinking to do. The cell was not uncomfortable. There was a metal toilet and a water facet. I tried not to drink water from the faucet because I thought there would be a lot of germs in there.

I could not imagine staying there for more than one month. I looked at the small window from the cell's door. I saw a young adult, looking to be around twenty years old and who tried to talk to me by using some random sign language words.

I didn't understand what they said because I couldn't understand what they were trying to say. I sat in my cell and started to feel hungry. I tapped on the window to get the Police's attention.

"Can I have food?" I asked.

"Yes," he said and handed me a bologna sandwich.

I could only eat cheese and bologna without bread because I felt like it soaked up the ketchup and mustard too much. However, I was hungry because I missed dinner and ate a few sandwiches. I was also at a loss about how many I ate.

I did tap at the window and tried telling them that I wanted to get out of the cell. The Police warned me that if I did that again, they would spray me with pepper spray. I was scared and didn't want that kind of trouble, so I decided to get some sleep.

A few hours later, the Police woke me up and asked me if I knew the person who'd come for me to pick me up. He showed me her driver's license, and I replied yes. He discharged me, and I felt more nervous to see the woman because she was friends with my mother.

When I was discharged, I saw the woman outside. Without saying a single word, I got in the car. We reached her house, and I was awkward for a moment before I started to get ready for bed. I had school the next morning. I wore the same uniform as last night. I felt anxious and embarrassed and walked into the classroom without a backpack.

Everyone was happy to see me when I entered the classroom, and my teacher said, "Talk with me in a private room."

She also asked if I was okay, and I replied yes.

About one month later, I received a letter from the court saying that I had to pay the fee and show up for the next hearing. Mom told me not to worry and would take care of it later. It seems like my mother and I forgot about the letter completely.

Until the Police actually showed up at my middle school and informed me that I was under arrest for failure to pay the fee and not showing up to court, requiring an advance date. The reason why we disregarded the letter was that we had no car to get there and hated taking the bus.

The court hearing was in the morning, around 8 a.m., and I was not able to make it there on time. The

Police didn't care for my feelings. They cuffed me, and I walked out. A few students in the hallway saw me. I saw one girl smirk at me, and she could tell that I was in trouble for something.

I got in the police car and soon went to the jail center. I had to stay there for a couple of hours until they placed me at the young juvenile detention center. Finally, the Police transported me and others to the center.

I had to remove my clothes and squat my butt, and the police lady had to do a quick check-up to ensure I had no tattoos on my body. The police lady said, "Ahead, get a shower quick."

She handed me a very small white bar of soap for my whole body.

"What about shampoo?" I asked her.

"We don't have any."

I wondered why. My hair still had the scent left from the shampoo from yesterday when I'd grabbed a shower at home. I still smelled fresh.

I was given a juvenile uniform to wear. It was blue, and they ensured I wore their shoes, underwear, shirt, and pants. I snuck my personal underwear inside without knowing it was not allowed, but I preferred mine because the underwear they gave me did not fit me and was too big on me.

I would ask them for it when I needed more later because I couldn't imagine wearing the same one for a week. I walked to a table and sat quietly. A few girls approached me and started to ask me questions.

Shyly, I told them I was deaf but could talk to them if they wrote it down on the paper. We sat there for hours, sharing our experience and why I was placed in that building.

I ate some Lays chips and drank Sprite. I was surprised they offered good food and wondered why it was not the same as adult jail. I looked at the calendar because I was bored and I never imagined that I'd have to stay here through all the holidays. I missed all the celebrations with my friends and family.

I really had no idea how long I would stay there because the Police did not tell me the details. All I knew was that I'd have to see the jury early morning tomorrow. When it was time for bed, I really wanted to join the two-girl bedroom because we'd become friends and chat for a few hours. I enjoyed getting to know a bit about them.

However, the Police did not allow me because they could bother me in my sleep. I do not know the specific reason why. I slept in the living room on the floor under a table, and the wool blanket made me itch. There was no mattress. I had to sleep on the hard floor with bright light.

I tried to sleep, but I failed because it was my first night there, and my mind was racing. I was very nervous to see what the jury would decide for me. Finally, I fell asleep. Around 5 a.m., the Police woke me up and said, "Time for you to get up."

They wrote it on paper, and I read it.

"Time for breakfast."

I got in line with both hands behind my back so the Police could count and make sure that everyone was there. I sat at a table with a tray and looked at the food. It looked pretty bad. I willed myself to eat some bread with jelly and an egg.

After breakfast, I was taken to the courthouse and sat in the backroom. I was a mix of emotions, and I wanted to cry. I was excited to see my mother standing there with her lawyer.

I wanted to go home and back to school and finish the assignments I'd missed for an entire day. The Police said I had to step outside of the front courtroom while they came to a decision.

I was led out with my hands and both my feet cuffed. It was hard for me to walk. My feet were a bit sore because the cuffs kept chafing against my skin and made blisters behind my feet.

Thankfully, the Court decided to release me, and I was given my dirty clothes from the gym I wore on the day I got arrested so unexpectedly.

Mother and I went home and rested for a day. I was so exhausted, and it had been a really long day.

Chapter 7: Gallaudet University

I was in my senior year in high school, and about to graduate, but right before I did that, I got accepted by Gallaudet. I was so thrilled when I heard this news!

I remember I was at a cooking class around late in the afternoon. I peeked at my phone and saw the email, the prospectus, and a letter saying, "Congratulations! You are accepted into Gallaudet University!"

I know I was not supposed to be using my phone during school hours, but I'd been dying to know if I'd gotten in or not. I also felt like time was slipping away. I applied to the university in late November, after Thanksgiving. It was late April, and my graduation ceremony was only one month away!

I did not ask for updates while I waited because I was too busy with homework and playing sports like soccer. Also, Gallaudet was not the only college I'd submitted an application to. I'd also applied to the Rochester Institute of Technology (RIT) as an alternative.

I'd been so restless that while in the classroom, I kept taking out my phone from my backpack and peeking at it.

It got to the point where my teacher questioned me about it.

"What are you doing?" she asked.

I told her honestly that I was waiting for an important email, and she suggested that I should wait until after school to check the phone. I agree, but about ten minutes later, I decided to check again.

I saw the notification from the email, so I opened it fast.

I jumped out of my chair in front of my teacher and classmate and said, "Yes!"

I threw both hands in the air and shouted, "I am accepted! I can't believe my dream has come true!"

Everyone congratulated me. I was so happy that I grinned all the time and was in a great mood.

A week later, I got another letter. This one was from RIT, and it said I was accepted there too. Now, I was confused. I became unsure about which college to go to and became overwhelmed, but I knew I had to make a firm decision.

Right before my graduation day, I got a call from Gallaudet during the award ceremony because I was awarded a scholarship for all four years there! That was what helped with my final decision. I also decided to go there because I did not receive any scholarship from RIT.

During the summer, I prepared for college, did all the paperwork that they required me to do, and shopped for clothes. I flew to Maryland in late August and stayed with my Uncle, Silas, for a few days before Gallaudet welcomed its new students.

Despite how happy I'd been before, I was extremely nervous now. Even when on the fight from Florida, I'd been fighting my nerves and dealing with fear. I was very nervous about starting this new chapter at Gallaudet.

To be honest with you, I really had no idea what kind of place Gallaudet University would be like. I did not have a tour of the place before and only saw pictures of it on the website. When it was time for me to go to the Gallaudet Campus, I was a bit surprised.

Once I saw what the area looked like, I paused for a minute or two.

'Do all the deaf from all states and countries go to this place?' I thought.

The place was huge. It looked like Gallaudet was more likely 1800 buildings together. I arrived and was assigned to the Benson dorm, where first-years and freshmen had to stay. I entered and was given a room key.

"You have a roommate, and your room will be on the fifth floor," I was informed. I took the elevator, feeling nervous and wanting to know who my roommate was.

On the way, a girl approached me and said my name.

"Yes? That is me," I replied.

She led me to my room. I met my roommate, who told me her name, and we had a short conversation. I unpacked my clothes and stuff and set up the room to look nice.

One week before classes began, I walked around campus but stayed mostly in my room. I started to feel homesick because I missed Florida's temperate weather. Washington, DC's weather in August tended to be cooler and damper for my liking.

One lady who worked in the Benson dorms noticed that I was staying mostly in my room all the time. She talked with Madison, who was my best friend and supported me all the way since I just met her during my senior year in January 2015. She encouraged me to be social with new faces and people. I was actually a shy person at the moment. Eventually, I met Axel, and we got to know each other very well.

During the first week, I went to all four of my classes: English, College Math, Introduction First Seminar, and social work. I didn't like the last class as the social worker because I was entered for lessons without knowing, and I was the only freshman.

I got the wrong classes from my advisor.

The next day I decided to see my advisor about getting one class switched to another. I met the advisor, and we discussed the plan. I asked her if I could get a Spanish class as a replacement, and they didn't have a problem. The next week I entered Spanish class and started regretting it because it was very difficult to learn because I had to write down sentences.

My perception of the class was wrong because I thought I'd learn more about the culture instead of having to learn each word. I decided to see the advisor again and wanted to drop the course to switch to another one. Unfortunately, my advisor told me it was too late, and I had to stick with my classes until the semester ended in December.

I was not doing very well in my classes and decided to start skipping two classes - Math and Spanish. I started becoming more interested in partying and drinking alcohol with unfamiliar people. One time, I drank a bottle of alcohol. I was drunk and on the eighth floor, and my poor roommate had to come up and get me down to our bedroom.

"It's Sunday night! Tomorrow is Monday morning. We have to go to English class!" she yelled at me as she dragged me to our bedroom. I talked to Madison on FaceTime the whole time. She was in Florida, still in high school as a junior.

My roommate was also mad at me for my antics when I was too drunk. I danced in front of about five men in my hallway and took off my shirt, too. Thankfully, she came to rescue me. Once inside the bedroom, I passed out in bed and woke up the next morning with an awful hangover, which I took to my English class.

I remember I was feeling so sick that I asked the teacher if I could go to the bathroom for a moment. I felt nauseous in the bathroom, like I needed to vomit but couldn't. I couldn't eat anything either because my stomach got queasy.

I decided to stay in the classroom until I finished the day. However, skipping my classes was beginning to affect my grade, which decreased in one month because I failed Math and Spanish classes.

I did not do the given assignments and did not meet the attendance required to pass. It was peculiar, though, that I got an A in Spanish class even after skipping it so much. It seemed that the teacher did not pay attention that I was not attending the class or doing the base assignments.

However, slowly, I started to slide into depression as I felt confused with how I was progressing in Gallaudet. One day, I was feeling particularly depressive. I was on my way to English classes and arrived too early. I saw my teacher going to open the door with a key.

I approached her, and I burst into tears. Surprised, she asked me what was wrong.

"I want to kill myself," I told her through my tears.

My teacher took me to the advisor's office and explained the situation to them. The woman there then accompanied me to the psychologist's office. Over there, she explained why they'd brought me.

"We are concerned about her safety," they said.

However, they didn't have the resources available to help me, so they called 911 to get me. I was actually sent to a psych ward and kept under observation and treatment. I stayed there for a week and started to feel better. I was diagnosed with bipolar disorder.

When I got discharged from the hospital, I returned to my dorm in Benson. Everyone was shocked to see me again and asked where I'd been.

"Where were you?" was the most common question I was asked.

"I was at the hospital," I answered, not telling them more.

I was walking to the elevator when a rude person followed me.

"I heard that you were HIV positive," they said.

I felt more distressed and thought, *'Why are they making up stories? Do they not know the true story which occurred recently?'*

I don't know where they got the wrong idea. There was a rumor that I slept with three men. Even if I did, I wasn't stupid. I would have used a condom. It was the most stupid rumor I had ever heard!

However, my mental health declined when I moved back to my dorm. The suicidal ideation continued. One night, I decided to self-harm and cut myself on my left thigh with a razor blade. I tried to hide it, but as I bled, I walked down to tell the Benson staff about it.

She got freaked out and called the Police. I got a trip to the emergency room. They monitored me closely, discharged me the next morning, and encouraged me to take my medicine daily.

While things got a bit better, I was still struggling, and during the last week of September, I made the decision to withdraw from Gallaudet.

On October 1, I left Gallaudet for good.

Chapter 8: Peroxide

In March 2016, I drank half a peroxide bottle in front of my dad's ex-girlfriend, Sunni. I did this when I was staying at her house for a sleepover and was not feeling the best.

Sunni called the Police, and an ambulance showed up at her home. She was very upset and embarrassed about what was going on. The Police forced me to throw up, but since they couldn't pump my stomach, I struggled to throw up using my hands.

I started not just to feel sick and nauseous but also high from the peroxide in my system. The emergency responders had to hold me up, help me walk out of the house, and get in the ambulance.

"Please come with me," I begged Sunni.

Feeling disoriented, I was extremely vulnerable, but I was glad I didn't go through this ordeal alone. Sunni came with me, and she was with me the entire time I was at the hospital.

The emergency responders wanted to get me quickly into the ambulance and take me to the hospital because they were concerned. I hadn't been able to throw up the peroxide. I attempted to contact my mother and Madison, but neither answered.

My mother's phone was disconnected from Sorenson's videophone, and Madison was at the fair with Farrah; she didn't read and answer my texts. I didn't know that then, though, and it only added to my sadness. In the ambulance, I felt so agitated and nauseous. The peroxide started to burn my stomach and throat, and the urge to throw up was getting stronger and stronger. When I arrived at the Fort Myers hospital, they put me in the corner of the hallway, not in a private room.

By this time, I was having severe stomach pains and could feel a burning sensation inside me. I wanted to throw up and screamed for help, and my body twitched. I couldn't stay still. Suddenly, I felt the all too familiar clench in my throat.

I knew I was going to throw up.

"I need a bowl," I told the nurse, and as soon as she got it for me, I puked everything out.

The nurse was pretty happy to see that I'd thrown up on my own, and the liquid was so clear and white. She rushed to get a doctor while I kept throwing up. My vomit was just liquid at this point, all over my clothes and even the hospital bed.

A few minutes later, the doctor finally came to see me.

"What happened?" he asked me. "Did you try to kill yourself?"

In that moment, I lied.

"No," I told him. "I did it on a dare. My friend told me to do it."

Because of that, I wasn't sent to the psychiatric ward. Instead, the doctor just sighed, grumbled something about kids and their pranks, and then discharged me from the hospital.

Later, Sunni told me that I was lucky.

"A doctor could have sent you to the institution and locked you up for good."

I know she was telling the truth. After all, I drank the peroxide and put it on the record like a red flag.

When I got discharged, I went back to Sunni's place. By this time, Mom finally answered the phone and came on a call with me when her video chat was working again.

She was so shocked when I told her what had happened.

"Why did you do that?" she asked me. Before I could answer, she added. "This is all Madison's fault, isn't it? Because she did not reply?"

She kept blaming Madison, but I told her that wasn't true.

"I did it because I was so depressed," I answered.

After I was done talking to my mother, Madison called me on Facetime to see how I was doing. She was shocked to see what I had done to myself recently. She was pretty concerned about me.

"Why did you do that?" she asked me.

"I don't know," I told her. "I was too depressed. I tried telling you that when I attempted to call you on Facetime."

Madison was pretty upset and showed she cared for me.

"I am sorry for not answering quickly when you had an emergency," she said.

During my recovery period, it was very tough. I stayed at Sunni's place for a few more days but had difficulty eating. I was trying to eat my veggie burger for lunch, but my throat was still pretty raw. Every time I tried to swallow my food, I could feel it throb with dull pain and felt a burning sensation.

I'd burned my throat from swallowing chemicals. Unable to eat properly, I felt sick because my body was weak. I couldn't sleep or eat and still felt the burning sensation. During this time, I smoked marijuana heavily.

I didn't care how my stomach and throat were aching. I just wanted to have a high to help numb the pain I was feeling. Marijuana is medicinal, and I believe that it can cure mild pain and discomfort problems to a certain extent. I kept drinking liquids like water, soda, and more to stay hydrated and avoid dehydration.

I did not want to return to the hospital for this condition. I started to regret not telling the doctor honestly what I had done or what had triggered me to do this because I truly needed to get therapy for my depression. But I never asked about it.

I was doing what I had always been doing and hoping that I'd get better, little by little, every day. I tried to be positive about what lay ahead instead of being depressed all the time. Slowly, my appetite got better, and in a few weeks, I would be getting a clean bill of health.

I was surprised because I thought that peroxide had caused serious, lasting damage to my stomach and organs. I didn't know what state my stomach was in because I hadn't gotten to get an endoscopy done by the doctor.

That was because I didn't want to get any treatment because I was afraid that I would look foolish doing it in the first place. My stomach and throat became a lot better in a few more weeks. I still felt sad all day because I was suffering from major depression, and my medication didn't help me.

Additionally, I wasn't sleeping and eating based on a healthy schedule. I tended to go to bed in the early morning at 4 a.m. and woke up at around 4 p.m. I was getting twelve hours of sleep but had thrown my body's circadian rhythm off.

I was also suffering from PTSD related to my incident. Every time I looked at the bottle of peroxide on the bathroom shelf, it gave me such PTSD. I'd have flashbacks about the incident that day and recall how I was rushed to the hospital.

It was a pretty scary experience because I clearly remember how I felt when I was throwing up and screaming because it felt like my stomach was on fire.

Chapter 9: No Father's Day

I grew up with an absent father, and I felt his absence more than ever on one particular day, Father's Day. Every year, on Father's Day, he was never there to celebrate that day together with us as a family. The thing is, my father had his own demons to deal with, and life wasn't easy for him either.

He was addicted to using drugs and had trouble recovering from his addiction. It was also what led to his mood swings and temper tantrums, which would lead to fights with my mother. He would get physically violent, and it would escalate to the point that he was incarcerated, on and off, for domestic violence charges with a felony.

I knew that despite his shortcomings, he still loved me and my little sister. He tried his best to change for us and planned to do so one day, but it was an uphill battle. He always had the odds stacked against him.

As a result, I was raised by my mother, so I always gave her a gift on Father's Day for fulfilling the role of my father as well. Living as a single parent, my mother worked hard to provide for me and my little sister. Raising a child on your own at a young age is tough because you have to work a lot just so you and your family can have the basic necessities like home, food, and clothes.

Yet, my mother did it all by herself, raising not just one but two kids on her own.

*****

When I was elementary age, I wished that my father was a good person. I did not like that he was always incarcerated or doing drugs all the time. I resolved that I would never be like him. I hoped that I would not take the wrong path and start doing drugs all the time like he did.

When I was fifteen years old, I reconnected and mended the relationship with my father again. However, things became pretty tense because my father wanted me to move in with him and share my custody with my mom. Even though I was happy to have him in my life again, I felt that this was a bad idea. He was a drug addict, had mental health issues such as PTSD, and was still physically violent to the women in his life.

He was still violent with his ex-girlfriend, Sunni. It was more serious than what he did to my mom. He broke her rib and tried to choke her. So, I didn't move in with him and stayed with my mother.

*****

He died on December 15, 2016, from a hit and run.

When I learned that he had passed away, I felt so shocked. It was impossible to accept that he was gone.

He was only forty-six years old. He was very young for that! The suddenness of his passing threw me into a deep depression because it left a lot of things unresolved.

For starters, my relationship with my dad had deteriorated again, and I'd stopped talking to him. I was planning to call him on New Year's in 2017 and check up on him to see how he was doing. I imagined that after making that call, we'd be able to reconnect again. However, I never got the opportunity to do that.

Sixteen days before the New Year, he passed away.

I had never even thought about the mortality of my father before this incident. He was only forty-six years old, and I thought he'd be around longer. I cried when I realized that everything I wished to say to him would now be left unsaid. Everything I wanted to make right with him was left unresolved.

I became so depressed by his passing that I decided to turn to drugs for solace. I started smoking marijuana heavily. In hindsight, I should have known better, but I was only twenty years old when I lost my dad in the first place!

Deep down, though, I always knew he would be gone before my mother because of how rough his life was. He was doing drugs, and he lived on the streets sometimes. In the evenings, I'd smoke a joint outside.

During my high, I'd remember our time together as bad. When my mom and dad were together, we saw violence often. He never changed his ways, even when they broke up.

It was my regret and guilt at being unable to resolve everything with him that really ate at me. I wished I had been able to talk to him one last time. When I found out that he'd passed away, I cried hard and felt regret over what I'd done.

I also grew to hate Christmas because December 15, the day my dad passed away, is only ten days away from Christmas.

*****

As I continued to smoke marijuana heavily after his passing to deal with the grief, I didn't realize how badly this drug would start to mess up my life. At that time, I was just smoking marijuana every day without fail.

It was only when my pre-trial court case started that it became a serious issue. One of the requirements was that I was supposed to stay clean and not smoke or consume any drugs, including marijuana, but I didn't. Surprisingly, I didn't get in trouble, so I kept pushing it.

However, once, my counselor for my domestic violence wavier asked me to stay clean for sixteen weeks to get a drug test, improve my social standing, and get a certificate. All of this would help my case.

Then, my counselor decided to give me a drug test. When she asked me if I'd done any drugs, I lied to her.

"I don't smoke weed, just rarely," I told her, even though the truth was that I was smoking it heavily every single day.

Taking my word for it, she set the day for the test. I had to go to a lab, and when I entered the bathroom, someone was there to watch me while I peed. The day before the drug test, I bought a detox drink to flush the THC out of my body.

The next morning, I woke up and went to the place for the drug test.

The woman watched over me when I went pee, and after I was done, she took the cup with her. I was nervous and hoped that the result would be negative.

The result came back positive for drug use.

I was *so* scared. I didn't know what to do next. I felt sure that I would go to jail. In the next appointment with the counselor, she was pretty strict with me. I had another drug test to do, and this time, I had to clear it.

"If you test positive again, you will go to jail automatically, with no explanation," my counselor told me.

After the second test, I passed with a negative. I was so relieved, but I still didn't learn my lesson. Once I was done with the test, I started smoking again. I didn't see it, but marijuana made a distinct impact on my behavior. I would become more reckless and not think clearly about anything. I would act without considering the consequences of my actions. All I saw were the benefits that marijuana helped me sleep better and it kept my PTSD at bay.

However, my habit was becoming a huge drain on me. I would always be broke fast because I kept buying weed from dealers on the street and blowing through my budget too fast. Nonetheless, I slowly worked toward freeing myself from the clutches of this drug.

Two years later, when I was clean, I took my father's ashes, which were kept in a bag, and headed to a fishing spot. I'd never looked at the bag before in my life. I'd brought it home but then stashed it away somewhere.

I never went to my dad's funeral because I was so overwhelmed with my life at that point that I didn't think I'd be able to cope with everything. The fishing spot looked picturesque in mid–March, with spring just starting to take hold after winter.

As the wind ruffled my hair, I poured the ashes into the river. I picked a spot where he loved to go fishing.

Now I know he is at peace with no suffering.

Chapter 10: Homecoming 2017

One day, I took a long trip and went to Washington, DC, by a Greyhound bus. My hearing friend, Theo, dropped me off at the Greyhound bus station. I felt a bit nervous about the trip because I was traveling alone and did not have someone with me.

It was a nineteen-hour trip. I had some snacks with me on the bus, so I felt a bit fine. I arrived in North Carolina the next morning with no sleep yet. My anxiety started hitting me up because I felt like something was going to go wrong when I arrived in DC and saw Gallaudet University.

I realized I couldn't turn back to Florida now.

I started trying to be positive. When I arrived in DC, I was excited, especially to see Madison. I took a Gallaudet bus to go to the Gallaudet campus. When I arrived, it looked the same to me. I took my suitcase and entered the Benson dorm.

A worker approached me and asked if I was staying overnight.

"If you are, there is a pink ticket that is for homecoming week."

"Oh, this is not my suitcase," I lied. "It's for my bestie. I'm helping her."

I had to lie because, on the way back, Madison realized that she forgot to request and get permission for me to stay for one week. Luckily, I was able to successfully stay in her room. When I finally got into Madison's room, I was exhausted. I fell asleep almost immediately, but it turned out to be a very short nap.

Thirty minutes later, Madison woke me up.

"Do you want to go to a party?" she asked me.

I was willing to get up and go. On Saturday morning, before the bash party, I had a feeling that something was going to happen to me and Madison. However, I decided to ignore it, but trouble seemed to follow us around throughout the week I was there.

Shortly after, I got busted for smoking weed with Madison and two others. Before that happened, I had a strong sense that we were going to get in trouble.

"We need to leave now," I told Madison, but she didn't listen to me, and then we got busted by the Gallaudet staff. Then, I had no choice but to lie to the DPS police.

"I stay out of campus. I don't sleep in Gallaudet," I told them.

"You have to leave even when a homecoming is happening on the same night," the Police told me.

Madison and I left the campus without my suitcase and were only allowed to bring the purse.

However, I had to leave because Madison was a student at Gallaudet. Nonetheless, we walked to the Benson Dorm, took the Gallaudet bus, and left the Gallaudet campus.

"I can't believe we got in trouble together for the first time with marijuana," I told her.

Once we got off the bus, we walked to the Union Station to get the train. When the train arrived, we were still unsure where to go and which train to sit on.

I felt so shocked that my intuition was right about what happened to us. Madison felt terrible and didn't know what to do next; we were still trying to figure it out. I didn't call my mom as I didn't want her to see the mess we were in. She would be upset and know her intuition was correct.

Before leaving to travel to Gallaudet, she told me to take my essential documents while I was packing all my clothes because she thought I would need them.

I thought I'd have to move when someone unexpectedly needed a roommate.

Mother gave me advice about my plan and how to pack everything.

"I don't feel that going to Gallaudet is a good idea. You're going to go to Gallaudet to spend time with Madison, but I feel like you will get in trouble."

*****

Sitting on the train, we were disappointed to miss the homecoming 2017 bash party. If we hadn't gotten in trouble, we would have been able to have a blast. We'd be looking back at how we enjoyed together at the bash in a very different light.

However, we literally spent the night on trains. We got off the train, stayed awake for twenty-four hours, and walked around in a DC town named Dupont Circle. Finally, tired and exhausted, Madison and I discussed staying at a hotel.

However, we couldn't get a room because we didn't have enough money. I only had a hundred dollars in my bank balance and just twenty dollars in cash. Sighing, we kept walking around.

I met a strange person who smoked weed mixed with Molly. It was my first time doing that type of drug. It felt so weird and tickled my body; luckily, I didn't like it at all. It's a good thing I got over it in two or three hits. I never did that drug again!

As we roamed around, I spotted many homeless people roaming around very late at night, like 2 a.m. Someone was also following us and made me and Madison frightened. Luckily, nothing bad happened there, but I realized we had to go somewhere instead of roaming the streets.

I almost paid twenty dollars out of my pocket for a club party downtown for Madison because she was only eighteen years old and had to pay to enter. I could enter for free because I was twenty-one. I walked inside the club without Madison to see what was happening.

Many people were dancing, and loud music was blaring. I wanted to join in and get lit, too, but it was the wrong time. I needed to save the little money I had for food as there was still a week until Friday when I'd be able to take the Greyhound bus and go back home.

So, early morning, at 6 a.m., we walked back to the Union Station and then took the train. When we arrived at the Union Station in the town where Gallaudet was located, Madison needed to go back to Gallaudet, sleep, and do her homework. I was begging her not to leave me because I couldn't come with her.

"I must go," she said firmly.

I was angry and flipped the fucking finger at her. I couldn't believe that she would abandon me like this. I felt so angry, and I did not know what to do next. I did attempt to contact my friends and family.

However, I did remember that my uncle Silas lived in Maryland Laurel, which was only thirty minutes away from Gallaudet. I thought that it would be safe and he'd be the most likely to come and pick me up, but he was out of town for my cousin's baseball game.

I texted one woman who was a one-night stand, but I could not contact her. However, I knew she was visiting Gallaudet for homecoming, the same as me. I had yet to see her around the campus and hoped she'd be willing to help me, even though I hadn't spoken with her for a long time.

When it was midnight, the Union Station was closed. I felt so shitty because I was entirely alone, and even Madison had abandoned me. I decided to leave after getting some McDonald's food and drink. I looked at my phone and felt so angry because I was stuck. I didn't know what to do next.

One week before the homecoming, I had a vivid dream about Ambri. I dreamt that we met at a bash party and just stared at each other without a word. After homecoming finished, we talked in a private room to apologize, and we hugged and forgave each other. After that, I woke up.

Real life definitely differed from my dream. But I hoped that the interpretation of that dream meant that we'd see each other. However, I felt exhausted and hadn't been able to sleep at all yet. My phone battery almost died because there was no charge.

I walked upstairs, looked around the store, and asked a restaurant if I could borrow the charger. A woman was so lovely and willing to let me use her charger. I tried sleeping on the table, but it did not work. I kept calling Nash, begging him to please message Ambri to come and see me.

"She doesn't want to come," he told me.

I felt so pissed off, big time, because I didn't know what to do. I just want a safe place to sleep in. I texted Ambri for the third time, trying to get her attention. I went downstairs to the first floor after the phone was full. I searched for a place to sleep.

I tried to sleep in front of the Amtrak train station in a chair, which was uncomfortable and too hard. So, I decided to sleep on the floor. The security guard saw me. He knew sign language and asked, "What are you doing?"

"Waiting for the train to come," I lied to him.

"Can I see your train ticket?" he asked.

"I don't have one because I lost it," I told him.

I decided to walk out and search for another place. I found it, but it wasn't safe because I had to sleep on the middle floor in the corner while people walked through the hallway. I slept there for fifteen minutes. That was all because I had to keep an eye on the phone in case anyone contacted me.

When I got up, Madison came back with her friend Judie. She bought me a snack and a drink. However, I didn't get to finish talking with her as Judie pulled her out of our conversation, and they rushed off to catch the Gallaudet bus. I was so perturbed that I threw the glass on the floor, and it shattered in front of security.

Luckily, he did not say anything to me.

"I want to kill myself with peroxide again," I texted Madison.

I planned to buy it at a Walgreens store that was inside the Union Station.

"Don't," she told me. "Security will be watching. You must leave the building at midnight."

That's when the Union Station closed. I just started crying, not knowing what to do next. As I sat there, upset, I met a strange boy who looked like he was a twenty-five-year-old. We exchanged phone numbers, and he started flirting. Soon, we were smoking some marijuana together.

I got high, and then he left me, too.

I didn't know what to do, so I kept walking on the sidewalk. Suddenly, I realized I didn't know where I was, but I looked at the phone map. The street was becoming darker as there were no streetlights. I decided to stop walking and turn back to a different way.

A stranger kept texting me.

"Beautiful, where are you?" he messaged. I didn't answer him.

I stopped near a tree to change my clothes and wore a longer dress because it got a bit cold. I was uncomfortable, but I was glad no one saw me when I changed my outfit. I walked some more and decided to stop because I was too tired.

My eyes were becoming blurry, and I could hardly read the text messages and the street signs. I saw a taxi that was parked just ahead. I started crying hard and waved to him. A man came out of the car.

"What's wrong?" he said, and I read his lip.

I explained to him by typing on the notes app on my phone. "I need a place to sleep. I have not slept for forty hours and got kicked out of Gallaudet."

"You can get a free ride to anywhere you want to come over and stay at my aunt's place," he offered.

"No, thanks," I said.

"Let me take you to the police station to see if they can help you," he insisted.

Finally, I took a risk and got in the taxi. I rode for free with him and prayed that I would be safe and not get harmed by him before I arrived at the police station. Finally, I was at the police station, and I felt relief.

I explained to the Police about what was going on.

"You can go to a homeless shelter," they suggested.

It was very far from the police station.

"Can I sleep here overnight?" I asked them.

"Okay, but you must leave the next day."

That was good enough for me. I slept in a chair with no blanket. The station was too cold, but it was safe, and I could leave my phone overnight charging with a charger that I'd borrow from the taxi.

The next morning, the Police woke me up very early.

"You must leave," they said. "You can't stay."

I called Nash and explained what was going on, and he texted Ambri, but she did not reply because she was sleeping. So, I had to go walk about in the streets. However, I felt better, but I was tired from not getting enough sleep. I opened my purse and ate some leftover McDonald's from last night, but it tasted horrible.

I decided to throw it away in the trash can. I kept walking around and went to the park. I lay on the bench next to the water fountain and thought about what to do until Friday when I could finally take the Greyhound bus and return.

I spotted the city bus, got up, and ran to try to catch the bus. I got onto the bus and tried asking someone how to return to the Union Station. I lived in Florida and honestly did not know where to go. Finally, someone helped me, and I returned to Union Station.

I stayed in the Union Station and tried to relax but I couldn't.

I decided to text the man I'd just met and smoked marijuana with him.

"I needed a place to sleep until Friday," I told him.

Thankfully, he did come to see me.

"Come with me to my place," he said.

As we started to go further and further away from Union Station, I started to feel funny about him.

"I don't want to go there, thank you," I finally said when I could no longer shake off the bad feeling.

"Why?" he asked. "Don't you need a place to stay?"

"No," I answered and walked away from him.

I went back to Union Station. Even though it was uncomfortable, this was the one place apart from Gallaudet that felt a bit familiar to me. Later in the evening, Madison came to see me and tried to help me figure out what to do.

I called Nash again.

"Tell Ambri to come here and help," I told him.

She didn't come down there, nor did she call me.

"Please," I begged her. "Pay half of the hotel because I haven't been able to sleep in more than thirty hours. I want to get rest, and I promise you I won't do anything and sleep."

Ambri was still in Washington D.C., but there was no room for me as she was at a friend's house. She'd be able to arrange something but she had to leave on Tuesday from Washington D.C. to Florida. Unfortunately, I couldn't wait that long.

So, that was a bust for me.

Finally, I asked my sister for help.

"Can you pay for a one-way flight to my home area?" I asked her.

"No," she said.

By now, I was really running out of options. Madison was also coming up with crazy ideas. She wanted me to go to a barber shop to shave my head so the Gallaudet staff would not recognize me anymore and I could slip past them.

However, I was hesitant about following this plan.

Another day was spent fruitlessly trying to figure out what to do. As six o'clock struck, it started to get darker, and Madison had to return to Gallaudet before the bus closed, which would happen by nine p.m.

Finally, my best friend Nash said, "You can go back to Gallaudet with the waiver form."

That sounded good to me, but there was no explanation of how to get a waiver form. Nonetheless, I decided to go back to Gallaudet and got on the bus to Gallaudet with Madison, who felt relieved that I could go with her to rest in the dorm Gallaudet. When I arrived in the dorm, the staff asked for my information.

"You got a DSP waiver form," they informed me.

"Well, I did sneak in to stay in Madison's room without a homecoming pink slip," I told them.

That was a big mistake on my part because Kali, who was responsible for the Benson dorms, declined to let me stay for three days.

I was so furious, and I left campus, crying hard. I did not want to sleep on the street, and I had no sleep for more than thirty hours. I went back to the Union Station and walked to the food court, trying to figure out what to do next.

I texted another person named Axel in Gallaudet to ask if I could stay at the Carlin Dorm. The plan was successful! And I finally made it. I slept in his bed. I was overwhelmed and depressed about the situation that had happened to me, but I was safe again. I stayed with Axel for three nights.

Then I realized that it was almost Friday, and I would get to go home safely with my family!

I also reminded myself that I must re-sign the yellow slip with Axel's roommate on Thursday night. Axel paid for one night for me to stay. My last night with Axel was bad because he pushed me to have sex with him.

"No," I said, leaving the room immediately because I was uncomfortable. I decided to go to Madison's dorm, and this time, I could successfully sneak into her room without having to be checked in or out by the staff. I was so surprised that no one recognized me during my walk around the campus, even though my name was now on the list of PNG, which meant that I couldn't enter the Gallaudet campus up to the one-year date of the incident.

The last night was spent with Madison. Very Late at night, we smoked together in a room. At the time, my guts urged me not to do it because I could be in colossal inconvenience if I was busted for smoking marijuana again, like what had happened during homecoming night.

Thankfully, that did not occur, and we went to sleep soon after. The next day, it was Friday. The next morning, I was ready to go to the Greyhound station. However, I didn't get to make it to get on the bus because I got into an argument with Madison's friends.

I was mad about what they did to me, not letting me finish the talk with Madison when she dropped off the food and rushed off with her to catch the Gallaudet bus. So, when it was time to go to the bus station and walk to the Gallaudet bus, I decided not to join Madison and her friends.

Instead, I dumped my suitcase outside and walked out. I saw Makel, and I vented my feelings. He let me stay in his room until I was ready to go home and figured out what to plan next. The bus ticket was non-refundable. If I wanted to buy another one, I had to wait for the SSI government money, which would come in on November 1.

In the evening, I decided to go to the DSP office.

"I'll tell them it's an emergency," I told Makel, who tried to stop me.

"Don't do it," he told me. "You will make it worse. Stay in my room until you find a solution."

Still, I insisted on going, so we went to the DPS office together, and they supported me.

"Everything will be okay," they said.

Then, a DPS woman entered.

"How may I help you?" she asked. "You can tell the officer."

The officer who spoke with me on homecoming night said I should have called him first before entering Gallaudet Campus.

"There was a waiver form," I told them.

They put me in a private room without Makel, and the officer told me, "There was no waiver form."

I was so confused I asked my best friend, Nash, who told him about the waiver form.

"I don't know who told me," he said.

When I told Nash the whole situation, he got upset with me.

"You shouldn't have missed the bus, which worsened the situation," he said.

After that, he hung up on me, and I cried way too hard, not wanting to go to jail. However, the officer did not punish me because I told them the truth.

He took me out of the Gallaudet campus, talked about the line that belonged to Gallaudet, and told me to avoid the line area. Makel was with me. He contacted his friends who lived near Gallaudet to get me a place where I could stay for one night so I could take the flight to Florida the next day.

My little sister paid for it when she found out what had happened. Luckily, the ticket was cheaper than the regular price and came up to only forty-five dollars.

"Make sure you board the flight and don't miss it," she told me.

I assured her I wouldn't miss it, but I really was in trouble. The next problem I was facing was insufficient funds in my bank balance. The 120 dollars I'd had slowly dwindled down over the course of the week. I needed to figure out what to do next.

Makel and I walked to his friend's house. They let us in, but the funny thing was that they thought I wanted to borrow an air mattress.

"I just need to stay one night," I told them. "I don't want to stay the next day."

They let me stay one night.

With that sorted out, we were still facing a problem with how I'd get to the airport.

"I'll walk to Union, then take the train so I can arrive at the airport."

"You're crazy. You will not make it on time," Makel told me.

The following day, I woke up tired. Nash called me to see what was going on.

"I can't make it to the airport," I told him.

Nash willingly gave me sixty dollars for the Uber so that I could eat on the plane.

Thank God, he saved my neck; otherwise, I'd go through worse scenarios as the number of nights I'd spend as a homeless person would increase.

Arriving at the airport on time made me feel extremely good. I was ready to head to my sweet sunshine state of Florida. In a few hours, I landed safely in Orlando, Florida, and I had never been more glad to be home.

Chapter 11: Salus Care/Arrest

In 2018, I was admitted to the Salus Care institution so many times that I lost count. In early January, I was admitted due to a nervous and mental breakdown. The thing is, I stopped taking my medication. Now, I know I should not have left my medication which I'd been taking for the last seven months, but I hated it.

I hated the side effects caused by them, and I also knew that my diagnosis of schizophrenia was misleading. I was severely depressed, and that too, with good reason. I'd just recently broken up with my girlfriend, who had a two-year-old daughter.

The child put me through hell because I loved her so much to the extent that I felt like she was just like a biological daughter to me. I was torn because I had to leave her mother and leave her behind. I was not happy in the relationship as her mother, my girlfriend, was insane and could not read or write at all.

I met her pretty unexpectedly in early November, right after the experience when Gallaudet kicked me out from the homecoming. Nonetheless, it didn't last for long, and the breakup took a huge toll on me as well. Couple that with the fact that I stopped taking my medication and I was in a bad headspace.

For this reason, I was admitted to Salus Care Institution. Right away, from the start, I knew that something was wrong there because they did not give me the right treatment. They kept giving me different medications every day because they couldn't find what was wrong with me. Before I could adjust to a certain dosage, they'd change it again, and my health would deteriorate.

I will never forget how traumatized I was at the Salus Care Intuition. It wasn't just the facility itself but the people there too. They had a patient, a man named Waylon, who looked evil to me like the devil had possessed him. His fingernails were long and unkempt on both his hands. He'd sit in his chair and just stare at me all day.

He'd sit as still as a statue, and the only sign of life in him was his eye movements. It was very creepy because I saw he had bloodshot eyes.

I did my best to stay away from him all the time. It was a good thing there was a 24/7 nurse supervisor in the hallway. Despite that, I was always fearful when it got darker and it was time to sleep.

I could not sleep alone or in the same room with someone because something didn't feel quite right about the place. So, I decided to take a quick warm shower.

Suddenly, I heard a voice, as if from God, say telepathically, "Please don't move. Just stay and close your eyes."

I did as I was asked to and wrapped my hands around me to protect myself.

When I snuck a peek, I saw Waylon, the guy who looked like the devil possessed him, enter the shower room and try to attack me. He looked very evil and like he wanted to punch me. His face was contorted into a mask of rage.

I started to scream at the top of my lungs, and it startled him. He left the room, and I sobbed. I guess he found his way in because there was no nurse supervisor outside. As I cried in the shower, a lady nurse entered the room a few minutes later.

"Are you okay?" she asked me.

"Yes," I replied.

Finally, I got dressed up and got ready for bed. I looked at the hallway, and from the door, I saw the nurse supervisor was there. I was so confused because then, how had Waylon made his way into the showers?

I heard the same voice saying, "Please stay where you are, do not get out of bed!"

So, I listened and stared at the lady who was scrolling on her Facebook page on the phone. Then suddenly, she stopped and decided to bang on the door, making me alarmed.

*****

One time, the doctor decided to give me a different medication. It caused my eyesight to grow worse, and I could tell it was not right for my body. I decided to take a nap in the living room. I pulled my bed into the living room because I was not comfortable sleeping with my roommate.

I felt like she would hurt me. That's why I'd rather be safe. When I fell asleep, I dreamed about a blood moon that matched the Bible's revelation; I woke up with sweat running down my whole body.

I called the nurse and asked for a paper and pen. I decided to write down what I saw in my dream. The next morning, I saw a psychologist and told him about the dream.

"That sounds scary," he said. Luckily, an interpreter was present in the room, so I knew what he was saying.

"You have to take a different medicine, Abilify," he stated.

I decided to take it and see what would happen. I took it, and then, thirty minutes later, I felt dizzy. The entire room was spinning, and my stomach hurt so much that I felt like throwing up.

The medication also made me hurt others for no reason. I decided to tell the nurse to change it.

I was kept with restraints on a table many times because any rude behavior was punished in this manner. They did not want to communicate with me because it was difficult. I was profoundly deaf. My behavior was out of control due to the inaccurate medication I was on.

I honestly did not mean to attack the nurse and then hop on the table. When I was restrained, I got out of control and started screaming. I tried to tell the nurse something, but they kept ignoring me. They just sat and scrolled on their phones.

I kept banging myself against the table to try to get attention. However, it was only making things worse. I looked like a deranged person with only my shirt on and no pants. The nurses and doctors gave me multiple shots on my butt. It ached, and my skin felt like it was burning. Eventually, I passed out.

When I woke up, I was still stuck in my restraints. I tried telling the staff I wanted to get out, but the woman kept ignoring me. So, I decided to hurt myself. I scratched myself with my nails. Finally, the nurse saw me and came running. Then she got someone to come and see. The other nurse wiped the blood on my neck.

Finally, they decided to let me go. I was so exhausted because I'd kept screaming to try and communicate with them!

****

When I was finally discharged from Salus Care Institution, I was back again in like one or two days because I'd had another meltdown. I'd been in my apartment and became panicked because I could see demons and other evil spirits as my third eye was very open.

I was very restless and scared. When I tried to nap on my mother's bed, I felt someone crawl toward me. I got up and screamed, but there was no one there. My mother was worried, and she decided to call the police to get me and bring me to Salus Care Institution again.

However, my third eye was too open this time, and I was trying to get used to my gift. Once, I took some schizophrenia medicine because my mind had not stabilized, but whatever he gave me did not match my neurotransmitters. The doctor kept giving me strong dosages without giving me a chance.

Like, he should have waited for a few days and let my system get used to it.

I still remember one doctor staring at me and thinking about what to do because he'd never seen my behavior. I kept laughing and trying to tell the nurse to do something. They did not believe me. They did not understand that whatever it was that was inside my mind and my third eye's opening were not easy - it mixed the signals for me.

****

On February 4th, 2018, my mother and I were invited by an old couple to come to their house and watch Superbowl football. When it was time scheduled to take medication at 8 p.m., I took around 400 mg of Thorazine. About thirty minutes later, it seemed that my mind snapped, and I went insane for no reason.

I think it was due to the fact that when I went to the bathroom and stared in the mirror, I could see a demon had possessed the woman. I looked away and kept both my eyes on the wall when I washed my hands.

After that, I did not want to watch the Superbowl and wanted to go back home. I became hysterical, and my mother tried to calm me down.

"Please call the police," she told the old lady. "Then they will take care of her."

By this time, I was going out of my mind, screaming and destroying the grass on the lawn outside. When the police came, I saw that my mother was talking to the police and told them that I had schizophrenia.

Then, suddenly, I felt as if someone was inside my mind. It seemed to come from my hallucination about the medicine I took at 8 p.m. I don't know, but I decided to get up and run and bite my mother on the arm.

The police cuffed me and walked me to their car. I screamed and cried hard.

I thought I'd go back to the Salus Care Institution, but there was no explanation given, and I was being taken to jail. When I arrived at the lockup, my mind was still not stable. The police took my photos.

The next morning, I saw the court, and the judge said, "You cannot contact your mother by order because you have assaulted her."

I cried hard and apologized. Through my tears, I said, "Where will I go? I have no place to go!"

The judge said nothing.

At about 8 p.m., I was discharged with all my paperwork. I read it, and it said that I had an appointment for a pretrial, meaning I had to take a drug test and show up every week, like Tuesday. I also had to make sure I was there on the given date, and I couldn't travel farther from Lee County. I also had to stay in one location at Lee.

When I finally got out of jail, I expected that there would be someone there to pick me up, but there was no one there. I did not know what to do next. The weather was cold, and it was raining a bit. My paper got wet and ripped.

I decided to throw it but then changed my mind, folded it up, and put it in my pants pocket. I kept walking in the dark as there were no street lights on. I saw a red light for traffic. I almost walked toward it, but my eyesight started to get blurry, so I decided to go in a different direction. I kept walking with my mind completely blank.

Finally, I saw the chain fences of a prison. The police officer walked up to me and said, "What are you doing?"

I answered him in sign language and said, "I am deaf. What is this place?"

He understood me and said, "It's a prison area."

He tried to write something on a piece of paper that he pulled out from the trash can, but it kept getting wet.

I wrote down Sunni's address so he could drop me off there.

The officer was nice because he gave me his blanket. I wrapped myself up in it and tried to warm myself. I arrived at Sunni's place, and she was confused about why and how I was there.

"The police dropped me off," I told her.

She knew I got arrested because she always looked at the phone arrest booking app.

She let me stay for one night.

The next morning, when I woke up, the first thing she said was, "You must leave. You cannot stay."

I don't know why she did that. Maybe she felt scared of me.

Finally, I got in touch with my mother again and was admitted to the Salus Care institution again. I went with feelings of trepidation. I started to feel very scared of taking any new medicine because of what would happen to my mind and the side effects.

Finally, my mother called them and told them off. She was angry at them.

"Stop giving my daughter different medicine because you will worsen her condition! You need to do a test before you suddenly switch things up."

Moreover, my mother allowed them to keep me there for much longer if needed.

"She needs to be there longer, like a few weeks or a month. Let her body adjust to the medicine."

They agreed with what she said, and my treatment was much better this time than the last few times. I stayed there for a week and a half, and I started to get better. My mood was more stable because they weren't experimenting with different drugs and dosages either.

When I was discharged, I focused on getting better and decided to take my medicine daily. If I hadn't started skipping it, I wouldn't have ended up in the Salus Care Institution in the first place.

Chapter 12: Hurricane Ian

On September 28, 2022, the Hurricane landfill at my hometown, Fort Myers and Cape Coral. I first noticed that the weather said it would hit North Tampa, but I already knew it would hit our area.

Mother woke me in the morning and said, "The electricity is gone."

Yes, we were pretty scared as we had to be in the dark now, but we kept the faith.

Thank God, Madison kept updating me about everything going on. She watched the news closely all day for our sake. I was texting and talking with her. Mother decided to take a short nap.

When she woke up, she was a bit disturbed.

"You spat in my face," she accused me.

"I didn't," I told her. She probably dreamed about the whole thing, and we took that as a sign; it was a warning from God.

We went to the window to see what was going on. I peeked through the blinds and saw how across the street, there was a steady flow of water; the street was flooding.

'*No way!*' I thought. '*Please don't come toward us.*'

Luckily, the water flowed right and left and not straight to our house.

I was scared because Madison had also warned me about it.

"It is going to be awful," she said, and she sent me some pictures. It was very traumatic and sad to see that the Fort Myers beach and Sanibel were almost gone, destroyed by an almost category five hurricane that was only two mph away from us.

The eye of the hurricane was very calm.

Still, we decided that we would stay in the bathroom for safety and avoid the windows.

Before that, I'd put my hand on the window and felt a mighty bang.

"Can you hear the sound?" I asked my mother.

"Yes," she said, and then she decided to turn off her hearing aid because she feared loud sounds.

We stayed in the bathroom all day until the storm passed.

My bathroom was tiny. I slept in the shower. I didn't have a tub in the apartment room because it was too tight. We also had a chest packed with supplies and food, plus I had one cat.

My mother and I did our best to make him comfortable. My beloved Sam was calm and happily stayed inside the cage. Sometimes, he'd lay on my chest for a nap and help my anxiety.

I used my phone all day and texted to learn what the update was. I used a small power bank for my phone, but it ran out too quickly. Three bars were out when the iPhone got full. I kept turning it on and off because I felt like the phone drained faster when the battery was on. I would check every hour to see what the update was.

Before the hurricane came, I got a severe, itchy patch of rashes on my lower stomach because of my anxiety. I thought I was having an allergic reaction to food or medicine. I didn't get a chance to see Hurricane Ian's eye because my mother did not want me to step outside. This was because of what I did when Hurricane Charley hit our hometown in August 2004.

I had tried to step out then, too, because I had no idea what a hurricane's eye looked like.

When the storm was over, there was so much debris, damage to homes, livestock, and other property, and flooding. My apartment also had no water or electricity. I couldn't take a shower. Mother filled four pitchers that we used to hold cat litter with water for the cats to drink because, after the storm, there was little water to drink.

Everything around us was contaminated with bacteria, and she didn't want the cats to get ill. The weather was cool and breezy, so we decided to open the window. That's when we saw that we were trapped and could not get out as two of the driveways were blocked by fallen trees.

Additionally, my mother's car battery died. It was awful. We were stuck there and had no electricity for around nine days. I could not charge my iPhone, cook, or run the AC. Thankfully, two days after the storm, we had water on.

But the toilet was not working or flushing due to the pipes being shut down or clogged. It got so bad that my mother and I had to wear a mask when going to the bathroom because it smelled bad, and we had to throw the toilet paper in a small trash bag.

I used a small flashlight to take a quick shower with cold water, but the water pressure was so weak that I decided to use one pitcher to wash my whole body. I hated the experience of living like this, but it made me think of how we tended to survive before, like in the 1800s when people did not have electricity.

I heard a rumor that power could return in a week or even take up to a month, depending on the damage suffered by certain areas. I was worried about my class which was due to start on October 3, and I had to post another quarter term.

However, I already withdrew because I did not know when the power would be turned back on. I was also still suffering from some bad PTSD that I needed to recover from first.

A few days later, the power was still out. I sat outside and stared at the traffic. I read a book to help my mind stay positive, but it was pretty hard. When it got darker, I always got terrible anxiety and flashbacks about the incident I saw during a hurricane. I also hadn't eaten much since the storm because of shock. I was petrified because I felt like we were so close to destruction by the storm, like what had happened at the Fort Myers beach.

I witnessed many ambulances driving pretty fast on Santa Barbara Boulevard Street in front of my apartment for nine days. The rescue efforts were also visible, including an army truck and helicopters. A food bank truck came to drop off supplies at the front driveway because the tree was still blocking the driveway.

I did ration the food and battery supply carefully because the debris was going to stay for longer than a month, and everything looked awful. The internet was also acting up because I couldn't access any website or social media platforms to see what was happening. Later, when I went to the nearest open Verizon office, I was told that nearly seventy-five-percent of cellular services had been knocked.

I texted Madison telling her how I felt and the dire situation that we were in. Thankfully, Madison and her dad came by. They dropped off the supplies we needed as the store was closed too. Finally, they also got someone to help cut the tree blocking the driveway.

My sister always came to check on us and helped us in any way possible. She'd take the power bank and charge it again so I could keep my phone charged. Thank God, she had a generator, so she had some electricity.

Then one day, my sister made a suggestion.

"Let's go drive to the McDonald's in Fort Myers and get a hot meal."

Even though I wanted to go, I was scared. I couldn't breathe on the bridge, and my whole body shook because I was expecting to see the carnage. When I finally got out, I saw what the debris had done. When my sister drove across, I was confused because I still saw water there. I thought that it had been emptied, but I was wrong.

When we arrived at McDonalds, it was already closed. Then, we walked to the nearest Chinese restaurant to get something to eat. I ordered a large meal, thinking I could eat it all, but I had some leftovers. When I returned home, I prepared the food and prayed to God. I took a few bites, and then I was done because my stomach was upset and anxious about what I saw as debris.

After the nine-day experience with no electricity, I was very traumatized and scared to sleep alone in my bedroom because it seemed too dark. Alone in the darkness, I'd lose myself in flashbacks and see all the flood debris I'd seen over and over. I could not believe that I'd experienced such a historical experience in my life and survived!

However, I am still thankful to be alive and to be able to text my friends and family. That's all I care about.

Chapter 13: Overdose

On January 16, 2023, around five p.m. I sat on my bed with the phone. I'd been feeling extremely depressed for quite some time, and at that moment, I just felt too overwhelmed and like I was stuck in my life.

So, I decided to set myself free from my pain and suffering.

I took around a 90-day supply of pain medication—800 mg of Ibuprofen tablets. The total dosage came up to around 72,000mg of pills, and I took them all.

The desire to commit suicide was completely out of the blue on that day. I remember thinking, *'It's Martin Luther King's birthday.'*

I just remember taking the pills from the bottle, shoving them all in my mouth, and gulping down as much water and Gatorade as quickly as possible. I also gagged because I swallowed too quickly.

Soon after, my mother entered the room. She sensed something was wrong because she heard the medicine bottle shaking sound.

When she saw the state I was in, Mom freaked out and cried.

"Nooo!" she yelled.

Mother called Ray because he was a nurse and called 911.

The EMS team arrived and asked me, "Why did you do that?"

I wrote down on a piece of paper, "I'm not happy with my life."

The EMS team said, "You have to go to the hospital."

"I need to go the bathroom before leaving," I told the EMS lady. She accompanied me to the bathroom, and then I walked toward the ambulance. On the way to the Cape Coral Hospital, the man put a heart monitor on me. I had already been strapped to the gurney with the belt buckle.

The EMS man had to make sure that I stayed awake and monitored my vital signs until I arrived at the hospital. I held my phone and read all the messages I'd sent to all the people I'd said goodbye to. I thought I would die because I'd ingested 72,000 mg of Ibuprofen, and it was harmful to the body.

I held my cross necklace because I love Jesus and wanted to see heaven. When I arrived at the hospital, I was taken to the emergency, but I asked to go to the bathroom to pee. I made a point with the American Sign Language to-wall sign that said "Restroom."

When I got out and walked to the toilet, I started feeling dizzy.

A nurse tried to keep me awake.

"You will die if you go to sleep right now," she told me.

Somewhere in the back of my mind, I began to regret doing this, but I also knew it would be too late. I sat on the toilet with the nurse's help.

"I can't pee," I told her. "I need a catheter."

Then I blacked out.

I woke up in the hospital bed feeling extremely high pressure and noticed a heart monitor on me. Then, I passed out again. A few hours later, I woke up in the ICU with the nurse supervisor. I felt so queasy and threw up.

I saw my mother text someone on the phone, and then she left because the visiting hour was over. Both my hands were tied to the bed railing.

"Why did you do this? Do I look crazy to you?" I asked the nurse.

"No," she answered.

Then I got a seizure due to the medicine's side effects, and I blacked out again.

When I woke up again, the nurse decided to do a sonogram on my stomach. I looked at the screen and looked away quickly because I was shocked to see that my gut was halfway full of pills. However, I realized that medication digested very slowly.

The doctor or nurse wrote on the paper.

"You need emergency surgery now," they told me. By now, I couldn't read and ask any questions or answers. I was rushed out of the ICU room and rushed to the surgery room. I was put on a surgery table and tried to get up and look around, but my body was too weak.

All I remember was looking at the clock for the time. I saw it was 8:45 p.m. Then the nurse administered general anesthesia to me, and I fell asleep. When going into a deep sleep, I felt that there were many spirits holding me, and I thought I saw someone who loved me.

After surgery, I woke up in the ICU and saw that I was attached to a kidney dialysis machine. A kidney dialysis port was installed on the right chest. I had two tubes attached separately. I felt a bit uncomfortable, and I kept trying to stay awake because God told me to listen to Him, and He would guide me. It was hard for me to communicate with the doctor.

"Can I have some water," I said.

"No," he replied.

I still took a few sips, and I fell asleep. God wanted me to rest. The next day nurse moved me to a regular room. I saw my mother sitting on a chair.

"I'm sorry," I told her apologetically, and she forgave me for what I did.

Mother and I learned that both my kidneys had failed.

"We need to run dialysis on her one more time," the doctor said. "If it is unsuccessful, you will be on the waitlist to get a kidney donor."

My mother was horrified to hear that. I held her hand and told her, "I will be okay."

I did have faith that things would work out for the best. Three hours later, the nurse took me to the first floor for dialysis treatment. She handed me a mask because the smell of the chemicals was strong. I felt exhausted, and I wanted to sleep but still stayed awake.

I didn't worry about my kidneys because I trusted that I would be able to recover quickly due to being young. When I finished dialysis, the nurse handed me a note that said, "Good news, it worked."

I was relieved to hear that and knew that I was going to be fine. I was smiling so much that Mother wanted to know what had happened.

"I cleared the dialysis," I told her.

She read the note and said, "Yes, thank the Lord."

I felt as light as air floating out of my body. When I closed my eyes, I felt like I was traveling in a tunnel. My room number was 237, representing that an angel gave me a message, which was peculiar. Madison's mother was also staying at a different hospital for her health condition and stayed at a room number like mine.

Madison was a bit emotional when she visited me, but she didn't show much of her feelings because of what happened to me. I talked to Madison a bit, like for like thirty minutes. I told her, "I feel like my body is floating."

I stayed at the hospital for one week and two days, and throughout the stay, I felt light and floaty. When I closed my eyes, I felt like I was traveling in a tunnel, and I had to try to fight to return to normal.

Sometimes, I thought I saw Heaven when I rested my eyes.

I saw many people smiling at me and saying, "Come."

The background was gold and so stunning. In my mind, I felt like I wanted to go, but I couldn't because I was going against God's plan for my life. I was cutting it short due to suicide. He already knew my timeline before I was born on Earth.

I stayed in bed most of the time because I was weak and was given so many IVs that both arms had many bruises. I also had to get bloodwork done often to check my potassium level. If I was deficient, the treatment I was being given would affect my heart.

I also had to meet with a psychologist.

"Why did you decide to overdose?" they asked me. "What is the date today?"

"It's January 17, 2023," I said.

"You drank peroxide at twenty years old in 2016, correct?" the psychologist asked.

I was shocked when I heard her say that.

"How do you know?"

Then I started to recall how when I'd blacked out in the toilet, the nurse had handed me my phone and asked for my four-number code on the iPhone. I did unlock it, and then I fainted. I texted someone and told her about it.

"I don't want to discuss my past because of the long story," I told the psychologist, and she respected me.

Throughout this time, my mother was with me. She made sure that I took the medication. I overheard my mother and psychologist talking privately in the hallway, discussing my plan after discharge.

I would be sent to Baker Act. I was too frightened to return to Salus Care or Royal Park because I didn't feel comfortable staying there and what they'd done to me in the past. When my mother told me, I felt concerned.

"I want to stay home, and you can monitor me," I told my mother.

I wasn't sent to the Baker Act because the nurse supervised me for three days. My behavior was normal, and I spent most of my time watching television and taking a short nap. I hated being on the IV all day.

My veins were sore because I didn't get to move around a lot. Once, I had a potassium IV bag and started to feel a burning feeling. It was so painful that I screamed. I tried to tell the nurse, but she told me to shut up. Later, she realized someone had restarted the machine, causing the system to get messed up, and the number had been higher than what I was getting for my treatment.

Finally, I was able to get back on solids, but I still drank and ate liquids like Jello and vegetable broth. I couldn't eat regular meals for five days because my stomach had been pumped to get the pills out.

One sweet nurse lady was made to make me tell her what I had taken. I kept saying, "I swear, just pain pills."

All I remember was overdosing on pills. Maybe I ate a crystal or a wall pin, but I had no idea what.

"I want to eat regular meals," I complained.

Finally, after almost six days with no food in my stomach, I had trouble eating because I often gagged as I'd remember how it'd felt when I took all the pills in my mouth. I requested a vegetarian diet and wanted to stick with it.

One day, my mother told me, "Your beloved Sam's illness is worsening. He seems to be dying soon."

I started to tear up and said, "Please, no."

In my mind, I hoped I would get to say goodbye. I did not want Sam to die on my birthday. I got discharged on January 24, three days before my birthday.

Chapter 14: Royal Park

I was admitted to the Royal Park late at night, after midnight. I saw the bracelet on my wrist had a date - January 26, 2023, one day before my birthday. I felt depressed because this was the second time I was celebrating my birthday in the ward.

I was admitted there because I was going crazy. My beloved cat, Sam, was going to die, but I did not know when. I hoped that it would be on my birthday.

"I put Sam to sleep on your golden birthday so you could make one special wish and remember him every year," my mother told me.

That was because Sam and I had a powerful and unique bond.

Sam and I always slept together every night, and he loved that I kissed and embraced him. I always spoiled him too much with treats. I loved to see him *meow* even though I couldn't hear his sweet voice - but one day, I will when I arrive in heaven. I was angry that I had to go through more loss, especially after experiencing an overdose and almost losing my life only eleven days before my birthday.

It was a very intense situation for me. I thought that if I died before Sam, we would meet in heaven on an unknown date – it would also impact the people who love him and me.

I sat in the waiting room at the Royal Park Hospital and was surprised because it did not look the same to me anymore. It was under construction and new staff worked there.

"Why have you come here?" the nurse asked me when I was being interviewed, but I could not answer until they got a Vri interpreter on the tablet.

The man who was my interpreter misunderstood me. I did stand up and said, "You should be fired because he did not listen correctly to what I said."

Then, I asked the nurse, "Where am I in the Royal Park Hospital?"

I was scared because I thought they had given me too much medication. That happened in the summer of 2016. When I was admitted to the same building five years ago, I did not return.

But here I was again, with unexpected circumstances about Sam dying and the overdose experience. My emotions were out of control, and I was overwhelmed.

I got up to the second-floor nurse in the early morning, who guided me to my room. I saw the bathroom door was soft.

I laughed hard and knocked on it. The nurse heard a noise and asked, "Are you okay?"

I answered, "Yes. I am trying to make myself comfortable and go to sleep."

"Try not to wake your roommate," the nurse said.

I sat on the bed and looked at the window. My roommate had painted on it, and it said, "Hope."

The word *Hope* gave me a message about the future. I believed I would have a good life ahead with love and family. Around seven o'clock for breakfast, I wouldn't eat because I did not have a special vegetarian diet. I decided to stand in the quiet room and look at the parking lot from the window.

I wondered how my beloved Sam was doing. I prayed and tried to be strong when I left this ward.

Lady Monica, who knew some sign language, came up to me and asked, "What is wrong?"

She had heard me crying hard when I sat on a blue chair.

"My pet cat, Sam, will die," I told her.

Do you know what they did after that? They gave me a shot.

I was so angry.

What the hell? Why did they give me one for no reason? I did not go crazy or want to hurt people. I had a few witnesses who saw the whole thing and knew what had happened. Plus, the nurse tried to give me a few meds that were not my usual. Daily, I kept telling them, "Prozac 30mg."

Stubbornly, they tried to give me a different one, but I wouldn't take it because it would mess up my brain. I am sensitive to any medication. Finally, I was given Prozac, and I took it to help me relax for a day. On my golden birthday, I was too depressed because I thought Sam would be put to sleep on my birthday.

I felt like doing something on my birthday, like going outside for fresh air. I had some chalk and drew with it. I wrote the words, "Golden Birthday" and my age. Some people said, "Happy Birthday."

I answered and said, "Thank you."

They wanted to cheer me up on my special day and knew about my birthday.

I had no way to contact my mom and sister. Only a nurse could make a call for me. I met my good friends, Asher, Jacob, and Ruth. We got to know each other because they witnessed what that place had done to me, and they felt disgusted because I was deaf and innocent. After dinner, I decided to lie in the hallway quietly, talking to God in the evening.

A few nurses grabbed my arm, rolled my jacket up, and gave me a shot in front of people. It was the most idiotic thing I'd ever seen! First, they tried to make me go to the room, but I refused. I knew something was not right. I decided to rebel and stay in the place I was in. It was traumatic for me.

I was not too fond of this shot because it made me sleepy, not knowing what it was called and what it was for. I still wonder why they wanted me to go to my room; maybe they would rape me because it happened to my sweet roommate. I did not know her name.

Who knows what could happen or how the nurse team would hurt me inside the room?

I am thankful to God that there were others who had witnessed what they had done to me. On the last day, on Jan 29, it was a very wild night because I met a new person, a man who seemed possessed. He tried to attack me and follow me everywhere. I tried to stay away from him. I was protected by a friend named Jacob.

He would tell him, "Stay away from her."

He had a big hand. I held it and felt safe.

I was told by my new friend, "I'll be right back."

I had to go to the restroom. After I peed, my instinct told me something was not right. When I opened the door, I saw the possessed man there, and he would attack me. I ran quickly to my friend. I was breathing heavily and told him everything.

That was not the end of it. When there was no nurse supervisor, the man entered my room one night. It was very creepy, and I wrote it on paper to show the nurse. They seemed shocked but did not do anything except for yelling at him.

"Can I use the tablet to call my mom and check on what Sam is doing?" I asked the nurse because my friend Asher could see and feel Sam was still alive and more likely weak.

The nurses asked the managers to allow access to the loaded app Sorenson and then make the call. It was going successfully, and I was too excited. This was the first time I was allowed to make to call since coming to the institution. First, I called my mother, but her videophone was disconnected and not working. I did leave a message saying sorry for what I did before arriving at the Royal Park Hospital.

I wore the red shirt honoring Sam when we took pictures with Santa in Pet Smart. Then I decided to call my former dorm staff lady who supervised me when I was in senior year. She was surprised to get a call from me.

"How is Sam?" I asked.

"Still alive and weak," she told me.

"Take him to the vet and put him down ahead of time," I told her. I gave her my PIN for the debit card.

Later, I learned that my mother was stuck with low funds and could not contact me.

All factories like hospitals and doctor's offices should be replaced with Sorenson for communication and better understanding with interpreter quality certificates. I hate to have a Vri tablet because it always has lousy connection services, plus some interpreters who don't know much sign language are hired for a job they are not equipped to handle.

That experience left me feeling that all deaf communities should be treated with as much equality as hearing people are. Deaf patients should be able to call if they are in hospital or jail, talk with family and friends, and have a lot of support from those who love them. Sometimes, we need it more than others.

Chapter 15: Technology

We are living in the 21st Century.

How can we impact the world with technology growing enormously daily worldwide?

When my third eye is too open, I can see what will happen thirty years later. The future will look like we're using robots for everything, but that will harm the Earth. People will be laid off from jobs because robots will take over – automation is happening already, albeit on a smaller scale.

People will drive their cars through self-drive, the advent of which are Teslas and other electronic cars. All stores, such as malls, gas stations, and grocery stores, will change to automatic self-pay checkouts via robots which is already happening in technologically advanced countries like Singapore, Japan, South Korea, and more to a certain extent.

Do you want our future to be destroyed by technology?

There will be no cash and coin exchange everywhere. We will force people into using card payments such as debit and credit.

People should be kept from using technology; it is a very troubling idea, given how we will evolve in the future thirty years later. Technology does come from the devil. I heard and learned that people already have chips implanted in their hands, and a lot of personal information is condensed into one.

I do feel that we need to get rid of it and stop.

We are not robots. We are humans created by God. We are not meant to use artificial chips in our hands, which can act like an open door. My fears are not unfounded. I have my own first-hand experience and many other reasons to think like this.

I was going to the hotel, Days Inn, to make a booking for a few nights. When I arrived there, I was shocked that there was nobody there to gather the information. Instead, there was only a robot in a big device with a camera and scanner function.

I was unsure how to start, but suddenly, the screen popped up, and someone who worked for Days Inn said, "How can I help you?"

I answered, "I am deaf and cannot write back."

Then the man typed in the device and said, "Please give your ID for the scan."

I just started to realize that this was not a deaf-friendly device because some deaf people will not know how to use it or how to write English sentences.

Why was there no live interpreter on the screen?

I touched the screen and typed, "I need to see someone who works at the hotel."

Eventually, a worker came to me, and we talked over phone notes. She told me, "You need a state ID, not a marijuana card, to verify the information."

I kept saying, "I do not have an ID."

I stayed in the lobby room to charge my phone for a few hours. I had a bible book with me, read a bit, and prayed.

At present, I see groceries have self-check machines.

We must go through this evolving time in the future very carefully for a few reasons. Having technology is very dangerous for the future and will negatively impact the economy and nature, such as plants and animal habitats. Today, humans focus on using a lot of technology in their daily routines. It is easy to hack someone's personal information. Technology needs to be paused for good.

Do you want robots to clean your home and drive you anywhere you want?

God created humans to grow plants for many reasons using our beautiful hands. In the future, it will become too strange when using technology. Humans will look plumper from being lazy, sitting around all the time with no physical activities around. We will have robots care for us. Also, everyone will be forced to get a chip in their hand; if we do not, we will get in trouble with laws.

Do you feel safe for humans in the future?

The answer is no.

Children's toys and things that are not tech-related, such as decoration, will not be present in the future. People will get rid of them as litter or waste. Some people will be willing to keep antiques to make money because of their value. You want the new generation to enter the world to focus on using technology, not old material that came out in 1980.

The new era will not understand how we use methods like ancient times because technology has everything at once. We use social media to connect with friends and family. I support a free environment. Not using paper because we have to save the trees on this planet and having a phone to video chat with those you love are poles apart.

We should reflect on technology and how we can use it well. Self-driving cars are a terrible idea because they can cause crashes, and fires due to something going wrong. Everyone who is a doctor and nurse can still use technology to save people for many different reasons, such as health.

For example, we tend to focus on technology in the future, but if storms such as hurricanes, tornados, and other related weather conditions can cause technology to shut down, how can we pay for gas and everything else due to the electric shutdown? An electric car needs to have plugs to move around.

Suppose a storm is in full effect; how we will survive as technology covers everything? If hurricanes come with a lot of rain and flood, it will cause any technology to become electrified, which could shock and kill people. This is a horrible idea and shows it is dangerous.

In one of my dreams, I want everyone to become vegetarian because there is a shortage of animal produce right now. It's why there are a lot of fruits and vegetables and plenty of grocery stores. Once, I saw a grocery worker dumping all the fruit and vegetables in the trash. Even though some were still good, some were decaying.

It made my heart ache that people weren't healthy and they like eating meat and junk food that is not fit for the human body.

In the Spring of 2016, I was at Salus Care Hospital. When the nurse handed me the lunch tray, I saw the paper that said vegetarian.

"Can I go outside?" I asked a nurse because I heard a voice from God.

He said, "In the future, all people will eat plant-based."

I got so excited, jumped, and used sign language to say, "Yes! Vegetarian All."

Everyone stared at me and did not understand what I was saying. They thought I was just psychotic.

I believe the government should plant fruit trees on the street for free for people experiencing homelessness, so they should have something to eat when they are hungry and they can survive. When planted in front of a restaurant or store, it would make everyone think of eating fruit like oranges or apples.

Downtown should install blackberries or raspberries to consume. It would be pleasant for wild animals also. That's why we should focus on a vegetarian diet. Additionally, many farm animals are abused before they are sold for meat. Once I watched the video, it made me sick because some animals were in such poor condition and even diseased before getting killed.

Why are we blind to this and buy meat from grocery stores that sell this meat on the front counter?

Once animals are short, how do we expect to get our animal protein for our bodies?

Some people will also have an allergic reaction to meat and develop high cholesterol. I do not understand why some people do not care about animals.

Why do you have pets like small animals such as hamsters, birds, and fish at home?

Would you kill them to eat?

I look at animals and consider them innocent, and they are all worthy of love! You can have plenty of fruit and vegetables on a vegan diet and plant substitutes to cook any dish.

Do you know that vegetarian and vegan diets have many benefits for your body?

When we walk to explore a zoo with any specific animal that has been caged year in and year out, do you think they are happy when people stare and take a lot of pictures? They make them feel tense, and they can do nothing but walk in a small circle and get stuck in front of a glass wall.

I heard a lot of incidents at Seaworld where workers were getting killed by killer whales because they felt trapped in the same circle. They've had to do the trick for selling show front tourists for fifteen years. In the future, all technology, such as cars, buildings, and more, will destroy nature on Earth.

How will plants survive and people eat if we keep using technology modems?

When animals cannot find their home once people destroy their habitats, it harms the Earth and animals. I see with my third eye how people will survive without plants when the world is full of technology modem.

If all trees are replaced, robot technology will kill animals and humans because robots can stay without air or oxygen. Installing solar panels to get energy from the sun for plant growth in a greenhouse will benefit us greatly, but it is still not a good idea because it harms nature, such as rocks, soil, and more.

Chapter 16: See the Jesus

In 2015, early in January, during my senior year, I had a very vivid dream. I saw that I was in heaven having a conversation with the Lord's son, Jesus!

He and I sat together and had a beautiful conversation. I saw a brown-haired girl come over, and then she sat down next to me.

"Pet the rabbit," she said, and I saw that she held a very pretty rabbit.

The dream occurred when I was living in the dorm at the Florida School for the Deaf and the Blind. When I woke up, I looked at the clock time. It was only 6 a.m. I went back to sleep and didn't wake up until 6:30 a.m. When I woke up, I was gasping, out of breath, and sweating.

I felt so disoriented that I was confused for a second.

'Where am I?' I wondered.

Then I realized I was in the dorm room at the Wartman.

As I calmed down, I recalled my dream and tried to remember how Jesus looked to me. I cannot describe what Jesus looked like. He has beautiful dark brown hair and brown eyes that are mixed with hints of green and blue, more like hazel.

When my dream was almost done, I saw that the devil got mad at me. I stood on a sidewalk that started to crack. I saw fire leaping out from the sidewalk and screamed in fear.

"Jesus, please help me," I said in sign language.

Jesus said to me, "I am always here for you, and I love you."

That's when I woke up, and to this day, I still have flashbacks of this dream! I never forgot that day. However, I was very scared of the dream the moment it happened. I was unable to find comfort in it. But today, I see the lord gave me faith.

It matched what I prophesized about the future.

In April 2016, I was down with a mystery illness that caused me to become worse. My whole body ached, and I did not feel like talking with everyone. I could not remember the day and time when this occurred, but I texted Madison about it.

"I am not doing well," I told her. "I think I have a fever."

"Why don't you go to Walgreens?" she suggested. "Go to get your temperature."

I did monitor it every hour, and I kept feeling worse than usual.

I decided to pull my bed out of my bedroom and put it in the front living room. I also stopped eating and drinking. Around 7 a.m., I got up and felt too weak to walk, but I did make it outside.

I sat in a green chair on the porch and had no idea what I was doing outside. I stared at the street that was busy, and traffic and cars were going by. Then, suddenly, I became dizzy, and it felt like everything was spinning.

My vision blurred, and I saw everything was red. I was scared and looked around, and it was still the same. I screamed loudly because I thought I was going to die.

Then I got a telepathic message from God: "Please, do not move."

I felt anxious because I had seen the number six. I kept looking around and saw the number seven. It felt like it was a countdown to something.

I texted someone I knew.

I said, "Please hurry 6,7. I love you. Plus, send me the picture of us together that I took at the Deaf School."

I kept screaming loudly while my mother was still sleeping inside. Only my neighbor was present. She'd come outside to smoke her cigarette alone and saw me having a panic attack.

When she reached me, she tried to take my phone. I refused to give it to her.

I kept screaming and said, "Please."

But I was saying it in sign language.

I was creating such a scene that other people called emergency services. Not only did a 911 team arrive, but there were also firemen and policemen. They were very confused.

The 911 team approached me.

"What's wrong?" they asked me.

I decided I wouldn't listen to them and flipped them the finger.

The only thing I said repeatedly was the word "Seven."

They did not understand what I was saying and soon became frustrated by me.

"Do you want to get jailed?" the fireman and police said.

I didn't say anything. Instead, I sat down and felt stiff, like I was about to pass out soon.

"Can I enter your home?" a fireman asked me.

I tried to say no by shaking my head.

Suddenly, I recalled a traumatic incident that occurred when I was five years old. I'd sleepwalked outside and had a mental breakdown at that time, too. The same scene had happened to me before. The fireman woke my mother by going into my apartment, tapping his feet, and flashing the lights.

Mother woke up and felt a little confused. She also couldn't help but have a sense of deja vu, recalling the time when I was five years old. Mother walked out and saw me.

"What's wrong?" she asked.

She felt that my fever had gotten high and encouraged me to take my temperature, but I refused. The 911 team decided to leave because I was behaving well now. I decided to return to bed to get plenty of rest and finally drank around a gallon of lime Gatorade to improve my health. After a while, I finally felt my fever breaking.

I could feel more chilly.

I do not know what the temperature was because I believe it was around 104. I remember taking the temperature myself before going outside. It had been 102. I do not know what kind of illness I had as I did not receive any treatment to improve it.

However, I heard God tell me telepathically how I could get better.

"You need to have meat again to be healthy."

I'd been a vegetarian for three years. I could not believe I was near death due to this fever.

Now I understand why I saw the numbers six and seven. They match the Bible's angel number and Seal revelation.

Another time I had a prophetic dream was when I was in Salus Care. I could see the dark red moon rising in it. I saw with my third eye that the second coming of Jesus would happen soon, but I don't know exactly when it would occur.

The dark red moon and the devil will look very sinful and destroy the Earth. It is important to believe in God and pray every day, no matter what. God is powerful, and I believe in Him. I know there is paradise in heaven. I can wait until it is my time and my turn to meet my beloved Sam there.

I miss Sam every day, and I believe he waits for me!

Sam was loved, not just by me but by others around me. Once, I posted a video with Sam in it on Instagram and was shocked to see that it had more than 14,000 views, and one thousand likes.

"You are famous now," I told Sam.

He did show up in my dreams with a message for me, too.

"You have to believe in yourself, write this book, and become a bestselling author," he said.

So, I'm here doing that right now, my dear Sam.

Thank you for believing in me!

Conclusion

After sharing my experiences, if there's one thing you can take away from this, I hope you never think of committing suicide, especially when you are in a dark place, or your life becomes difficult. Having experienced it firsthand, I can say that ending your life may look like the solution to the problem you're experiencing, but it is not.

You might feel like you're all alone, but you are not. There's always a helping end or a shoulder to lean on. This doesn't always have to be in the form of your friends, loved ones, or family. It could be your beloved pet or even God. God never leaves you alone. Even when it may look like it, you just need to see the signs He is offering.

Look at my story and see just how many times I attempted suicide. I felt like I was all alone and could no longer bear the pain, but I failed each time. I am truly grateful because I would not be here, writing my story and sharing it with the world otherwise. God wanted me to see that there was still a place here on Earth, and He has the same intention for you.

God truly loves you and already has a plan for you.

Remember that suicide will not help you to solve the problem immediately. Instead, you're making a grave mistake when you forget how painful this step is for you and your family. You will wreck their hearts, especially when your family and friends who love you so much find out about it!

For those who have lost loved ones or others to suicide, it is not because God had no plans for them or because they made a mistake. It's just the darkness and pain that surrounded them was too much for them to bear. That's one of the dangers of suicidal ideation. It can pull a person in, making them feel like there's no light at the end of the tunnel.

I truly grieve for those who succumbed to this ideation because it shows me how difficult their lives must have been. I hope they're in heaven and can find the rest, peace, and love they truly deserve.

I believe that we still have a long way to go to overcome suicidal ideation and its challenges. The main way we can start to do this is to change our overall outlook on life. Start seeing it as a beautiful learning process to be our best selves. It can be difficult, but I know that it can be done.

We can all work toward a purpose to accomplish, no matter how big or small. Don't give in to self-doubt, negativity, or pessimism, even if it looks hopeless. Remember, *"A journey of a thousand miles begins with a single, small step."*

Think of a dream in your life path and become successful in what you want!

In writing this book, I was able to accomplish my dream, but it was not an easy task at all. Many times, I wanted to give up and faced difficulty, but I want to thank the people in my life right now who believe that I will become a best-selling author and be able to influence people who experience depression positively.

I refuse to dim my light and hide the times when I was drowning in the darkness because doing that would entail silencing my voice, which would be dangerous to my sense of self. Now, you might understand why, even when I thought my life was completely over and all I saw was darkness, I was able to make my way to the light.

I am a shining beacon, a testament that you can make your way out of the black pit of depression. I am here as the first author of my book.

I know this is not the end of the journey because I will have a second book in the future. I want to share the stories, secrets, and sorrow I kept in my heart. I want to show others that suicide is worthless for me because I started being happy with my life and want to become a therapist for deaf children or adults.

Through my own experiences, I want to share the challenges we face and how we can overcome them to have a happy and meaningful life.

As I end the book, I want to share my favorite Bible verses so others may gain the same serenity, faith, and hope I did from them.

"I can do all things through Christ who strengthens me." **Philippians 4:13**

"For I know the plans I have for you," declares the Lord. *"Plans to prosper you and not to harm you, plans to give you hope and a future."* **Jeremiah 29:11**

"Yes, my soul, find rest in God; my hope comes from him. Truly, He is my rock and my salvation; he is my fortress, I will not be shaken." **Psalm 62:5–6**

"Even though I walk through the valley of the shadow of death, I will fear no evil, for you are with me; your rod and your staff, they comfort me." **Psalm 23:4**

"Peace I leave with you; my peace I give to you. Not as the world gives do I give to you. Let not your hearts be troubled, neither let them be afraid." **John 14:17**